WOMEN OF THE SPIRIT BIBLE STUDY

Vol. III: All About Trials

JOY HANEY

All Scripture quotations are from the King James Version of the Holy Bible unless otherwise noted.

Women of the Spirit Bible Study by Joy Haney
Volume III: All About Trials
Published by Radiant Life Publications
Stockton, California
Second Printing May 1998

Printed in the United States of America

Library of Congress Catalog Number 94-68446
ISBN# 1-880969-19-X

Introduction

This Bible Study, *Volume III: All About Trials,* is indeed a miracle volume. I woke up at 2:00 Saturday morning on January 6, 1995 and scribbled down the outline for this Bible study, and then went back to sleep.

The next morning the Lord gave me such inspiration that the outline for seven lessons were finished by that night, and the eighth was finished early Sunday morning. This was a divine miracle from God and all glory is given to him. He chose to let inspiration flow like a river through me that day; it just never stopped.

I stand in awe and amazement at His wonderful power and glory. My prayer is that your eyes will be opened to a new dimension in God as you begin to study this volume. May the blessing of the Lord be upon you and may His face shine upon you as you study about His Word.

Women of the Spirit Bible Study
Volume III: All About Trials

Table of Contents

Lessons:

Women of the Spirit Bible Study
Trials
Lesson I

I. Trials

A. What is a Trial?

1. Webster's Definitions:

   a. Trial means the action or process of trying or putting to the proof; a test. It also means the state or fact of being tried by suffering; hence, that which so tries or afflicts; a cross; tribulation. It is a source of vexation.

   b. Afflict means to inflict some great injury or hurt upon, causing continued pain or mental distress; to trouble grievously.

   c. Tribulation means distress or suffering; to press or afflict.

2. Jesus said in John 16:33, “These things I have spoken unto you, that in me ye might have peace. In the world ye shall have tribulation: but be of good cheer; I have overcome the world.”

a. *"You are under pressure, but take courage."*
   Berkeley Version of the New Testament
b. *"You have affliction, but keep up your courage."*
   Richard Francis Weymouth
c. *"You will find suffering."*
   E.V. Rieu
d. *"You will find trouble."*
   The Twentieth Century New Testament

3. It is an established fact, you will have trials and tribulation in the Christian walk.

B. Why are there trials?

1. "Troubles are often the tools by which God fashions us for better things." H.W. Beecher

2. I Peter 5:10 says, "But the God of all grace, who hath called us unto his eternal glory by Christ Jesus, after that ye have suffered a while, make you perfect, stablish, strengthen, settle you."

   a. Trials ocur in your life for the following reasons:

      i. To perfect you
      ii. To stablish you
      iii. To strengthen you
      iv. To settle you

   b. Webster's Definitions:

      i. To perfect means to make complete, sound, flawless, exact; not deficient, defective, or faulty.

      ii. To stablish is the archaic aphetic form of establish. Establish means to make stable or firm; to fix immovable or firmly.

ngthen means to make, grow, or
e stronger.

le means to place in a position, to
; to make firm, steady, or stable; to
ots.

ork in you that will help make you
ey help you become the woman that
you to be. Trials make you strong,
and immovable in your faith, and they
ne with the glory of the Lord.

increasing, earnest prayer
, for light, for strength to bear
rtion of the weight of care
ushes into dumb despair
lf the human race.
Henry Wadsworth Longfellow

ii. "...Be strong in the Lord, and in the power of his might" (Ephesians 6:10).

3. Trials work patience in you.

a. Romans 5:3-4 says, "And not only so, but we glory in tribulations also: knowing that tribulation worketh patience; And patience, experience; and experience, hope."

b. James 1:4 says, "Knowing this, that the trying of your faith worketh patience."

i. Patience means to bear or endure trials without complaint; longsuffering. It means to be expectant with calmness, without discontent, undisturbed by failures, obstacles, or delays; persevering.

ii. If you are patient, longsuffering, contented, calm, and able to endure all things without complaint or causing a disturbance to those around you or within yourself while you are going through a trial, then very likely you do not need trials.

c. *Learn to wait. It is life's hardest lesson*
Conned, perchance, through blinding tears;
While the heart throbs sadly echo
To the tread of passing years.
Learn to wait-hope's slow fruition;
Faint not, though the way seems long;
There is joy in each condition;
Hearts through suffering may grow strong.
Thus a soul untouched by sorrow
Aims not at a higher state;
Joy seeks not a brighter morrow;
Only sad hearts learn to wait.

4. Trials are appointed for every Christian. Read I Thessalonians 3:3-13.

a. The following verses are emphasized:

i. Verse 3 says, "That no man should be moved by these afflictions: for yourselves know that we are appointed thereunto."

ii. Verse 4 says, "For verily, when we were with you we told you before that we should suffer tribulation; even as it came to pass, and ye know."

b. Disappointments and afflictions will come, but Psalm 34:19 says, "Many are the afflictions of the righteous: but the Lord delivereth him out of them all."

c. "Disappointment to a noble soul is what cold water is to burning metal; it strengthens, tempers, intensifies, but never destroys it."
Eliza Tabor

C. Trials are too precious to waste.

1. I Peter 1:7 says, "That the trial of your faith, being much more precious than of gold that perisheth, though it be tried with fire, might be found unto praise and honour and glory at the appearing of Jesus Christ."

2. Job 23:10 says, "But he knoweth the way that I take: when he hath tried me, I shall come forth as gold."

a. *"The deeper the trial, the richer the gold."*

b. *"I thank God for my handicaps, for through them, I have found myself, my work, and my God."*
Helen Keller

3. Alexander MacLaren of Manchester said this about trials. "Sorrows blow us to His breast, as a strong wind might sweep a man into some refuge from itself. I am sure there are many who can thankfully attest that they were brought nearer to God by some short, sharp sorrow than by long days of prosperity. Take care that you do not waste your sorrows; that you do not let the precious gifts of disappointment, pain, loss, loneliness, ill health, or similar afflictions that come into your daily life mar you instead of mending you. See that they send you nearer to God, and not that they drive you farther from Him."

D. You cannot enter into the kingdom of God without trials and tribulations. You will have trials.

1. Acts 14:22 says, "Confirming the souls of the disciples, and exhorting them to continue in the faith, and that we must through much tribulation enter into the kingdom of God."

2. Read Hebrews 12:5-11. Sometimes trials are the Lord's chastening, which seems hard to understand, but it is for our good.

a. Note especially verses 10-11.

i. Verse 10 says, "For they verily for a few days chastened us after their own pleasure; but he for our profit, that we might be partakers of his holiness."

ii. Verse 11 says, "Now no chastening for the present seemeth to be joyous, but grievous: nevertheless afterward it yieldeth the peaceable fruit of righteousness unto them which are exercised thereby."

b. *"The gem cannot be polished without friction, nor man perfected without trials."*

Chinese Proverb

3. John 16:33 says, "These things I have spoken unto you, that in me ye might have peace. In the world ye shall have tribulation: but be of good cheer; I have overcome the world."

4. Hebrews 6:12 says, "That ye be not slothful, but followers of them who through faith and *patience* inherit the promises." Patience is learned through trials as taught in Romans 5:3.

E. Trials are for refining.

1. Read the following Scriptures:

a. "But he knoweth the way that I take: when he hath tried me, I shall come forth as gold" (Job 23:10).

b. "For thou, O God, hast proved us: thou hast tried us, as silver is tried" (Psalm 66:10).

c. "Beloved, think it not strange concerning the fiery trial, which is to try you" (I Peter 4:12).

d. "Behold, I have refined thee, but not with silver; I have chosen thee in the furnace of affliction" (Isaiah 48:10).

e. "...for he is like a refiner's fire, and like fullers' soap: and he shall sit as a refiner and purifier of silver: and he shall *purify the sons of Levi*, and purge them as gold and silver, that they may offer unto the Lord an offering in righteousness" (Malachi 3:2-3).

i. The sons of Levi participated in the priestly duties of the Old Testament. In the New Testament, Jesus became the great High Priest, who offered himself as a sacrifice. This enabled all of those who receive the Holy Ghost to enter into the Holy of holies and approach the throne of God for themselves instead of going through a priest.

ii. The Christian becomes a priest unto God according to the book of Revelation.

iii. Revelation 1:5-6 says, "And from Jesus Christ, who is the faithful witness, and the first begotten of the dead, and the prince of the kings of the earth. Unto him that loved us, and washed us from our sins in his own blood, And hath made us kings and priests unto God."

2. Refining is always a painful process.

a. *"Affliction, like the iron-smith, shapes as it smites."*

Christian Nestell Bovee

b. *"As threshing separates the wheat from the chaff, so does affliction purify virtue."*

Richard E. Burton

c. *"Affliction comes to us, not to make us sad but sober; not to make us sorry but wise."*

Henry Ward Beecher

d. *"Out of suffering have emerged the strongest souls."*

Edwin Hubbel Chapin

3. James McConkey writes the following remarks in the article entitled, *Chastening*: "Whom the Lord loveth He chasteneth (Hebrews 12:6). A visitor was watching a silversmith heating the silver in his crucible. Hotter and hotter grew the fires. All the while the smith was closely scanning the crucible. Presently the visitor said: 'Why do you watch the silver so closely? What are you looking for?' 'I am looking for my face,' was the answer. 'When I see my own image in the silver, then I stop. The work is done.' Why did the silversmith light the fires under the silver? To purify and perfect it. Is God's child-training an executioner visiting upon us the wrath of God?

"Nay, it is rather a cleansing angel pouring forth upon us the love of God. The furnace, the suffering, the agony of child-training, what do they mean? God is looking for a face! It is the face of Jesus Christ. And God's great purpose is that Christ should be formed in us."

F. Trials soften us and teach us to have compassion.

1. "*The dew of compassion is a tear.*"
   Lord Bryon

2. You really do not know how to help people *fully* until you have felt pain or sorrow yourself. When you go through a trial and are comforted by God, it is required of you to then comfort those who are going through the same trial or similar trouble. You have been there and can relate to their problem and help them to triumph over the trial.

3. Read I Corinthians 1:4-6.

   a. "[God] comforteth us in all our tribulation, that we may be able to comfort them which are in any trouble, by the comfort wherewith we ourselves are comforted of God."

   b. "For as the sufferings of Christ abound in us, so our consolation also aboundeth by Christ."

   c. "And whether we be afflicted, it is for your consolation and salvation, which is effectual in the enduring of the same sufferings which we also suffer: or whether we be comforted, it is for your consolation and salvation."

4. "A master of metaphor has made the complaining wax speak thus: 'Unaccountable, this!' said the wax, as from the flame it dropped melting upon the paper beneath. 'Do not grieve,' said the paper, 'I am sure it is all right.'

'I was never in such agony!' exclaimed the wax, still dropping.
'It is not without a good design, and will end well,' replies the paper.
"The wax was unable to reply at once, and when it again looked up it bore a beautiful impression, the counterpart of the seal which had been applied to it.
'Ah, I understand now!' said the wax, no longer in suffering. 'I was softened in order to receive this lovely, durable impress.'"

Author unknown

G. You are made perfect through suffering.

1. Psalm 119:67 says, "Before I was afflicted I went astray: but now have I kept thy word."

2. Psalm 119:71 says, "It is good for me that I have been afflicted; that I might learn thy statutes."

3. Hebrews 2:10 says, "For it became him, for whom are all things, and by whom are all things, in bringing many sons unto glory, to make the captain of their salvation perfect through sufferings."

H. The suffering that accompanies trials teach obedience.

1. Hebrews 5:8-9 says of Jesus, "Though he were a Son, yet learned he obedience by the things which he suffered; and being made perfect, he became the author of eternal salvation unto all them that obey him."

2. James H. McConcey tells the story about a woman who was summering in Switzerland. One day she started out for a stroll. Presently, as she climbed the mountain-side, she came to a shepherd's fold. She walked to the door and looked in, and there sat the shepherd. Around him lay his flock. Near at hand, on a pile of straw, lay a single sheep. It seemed to be in suffering. Scanning it closely,

the woman saw that its leg was broken. At once her sympathy went out to the suffering lamb. She looked up inquiringly to the shepherd. "How did it happen?" she said. To her amazement, the shepherd answered: "Madam, I broke that sheep's leg." A look of pain swept over the visitor's face. Seeing it, the shepherd went on: "Madam, of all the sheep in my flock, this one was the most wayward. It never would obey my voice. It never would follow in the pathway in which I was leading the flock. It wandered to the verge of many a perilous cliff and dizzy abyss. And, not only was it disobedient itself, but it was ever leading the other sheep of my flock astray. I had before had experience with sheep of this kind. So I broke its leg. The first day I went to it with food, it tried to bite me. I let it lie alone for a couple of days. Then, I went back to it. Now, it not only took food, but licked my hand, and showed every sign of submission and even affection. And now let me tell you something. When this sheep is well, as it soon will be, it will be the model sheep of my flock. No sheep will hear my voice so quickly. None will follow so closely at my side. Instead of leading its mates astray, it will now be an example and a guide for the wayward ones, leading them, with itself, in the path of obedience to my call. In short, a complete transformation will have come into the life of this wayward sheep. It has learned obedience through its suffering."

I. Trials are to make you know the Lord better.

1. Paul said in Philippians 3:10, "That I may know him, and the power of his resurrection, and the fellowship of his sufferings, being made conformable unto his death."

a. Trials make you more conformable to the cross.

i. Conformable means that which conforms, being like or in agreement, harmony, or obedient.

ii. The following Scriptures show that obedience brings power to a person's life.

iii. When Paul addressed special people in Romans 16 and commended them, he emphasized their obedience. Verse 17 says, "For your obedience is come abroad to all men."

iv. Paul addressed Philemon with much the same commendation. Philemon 1:21 says, "Having confidence in thy obedience I wrote unto thee, knowing that thou wilt also do more than I say."

b. When you are in the trial, you probably feel like retreating, hiding, or running away. This is the time to learn more about the Lord and to do mighty things in God.

i. Daniel 11:32 says, "But the people that do know their God shall be strong, and do exploits."

ii. The trial is no time to shrivel up and die, but it is a time to reach out and win others to Christ. "They that be wise shall shine as the brightness of the firmament; and they that turn many to righteousness as the stars for ever and ever" (Daniel 12:3). But remember in order for something to shine there must be buffing and polishing. Trials are supposed to make you shine, not make you retreat!

Lesson I Quiz

1. What is a trial?

2. Why are there trials? Give biblical answers.

   a.

   b.

   c.

   d.

   e.

3. Explain the refining process.

4. Why does God use suffering to teach obedience?

5. How should you respond in a trial?

Women of the Spirit Bible Study
Your Attitude
in the Trial
Lesson II

II. Your Attitude in the Trial

A. Trials can either make you bitter toward God or people, or they can cause you to become a better person.

1. Read Matthew 13:18-23. Note especially verse 21. It says, "Yet hath he not root in himself, but dureth for a while: for when tribulation or persecution ariseth because of the word, by and by he is offended."

   a. Tribulation or suffering can cause a person to become offended.

   b. In Matthew 11:2-6 Jesus told his disciples to tell John that although he was still in prison, there were great miracles taking place elsewhere. He ended with these words. "And blessed is he, whosoever shall not be offended in me" (Matthew 11:6).

c. You may not understand why you are allowed to suffer, while others are seemingly enjoying great blessings, but you must keep your heart from being offended.

d. To offend means to cause dislike, anger, or vexation. To be offended means to feel hurt or resentful towards the one that wounded you.

2. Your wounds can cause offense or create a pearl.

   a. Dr. Edward T. Sullivan preached from the Scripture in Revelation 21:21 which says, "And the twelve gates were twelve pearls." His message was entitled, *Every Gate a Pearl*. He said, "Every entrance into the heavenly life is through a pearl! What is a pearl? A wound is made in a shell. A grain of sand gets imbedded in the wound. And all the resources of repair are rushed to the place where the breach has been made. When the breach has been closed, and the process of repair is complete, a pearl is found closing the wound. The break calls forth unsuspected resources of the shell and a beauty appears that is not otherwise brought out. A pearl is a healed wound. No wound, no pearl."

   b. The best way not to become offended or bitter toward God or others is to devour the Word of God. Read the following Scriptures:

      i. Psalm 119:105 & 107 says, "Thy word is a lamp unto my feet, and a light unto my path. I am afflicted very much: quicken me, O Lord, according unto thy word."

ii. "Thy word have I hid in mine heart, that I might not sin against thee" (Psalm 119:11).

iii. "My soul melteth for heaviness: strengthen thou me according unto thy word" (Psalm 119:28).

iv. "This is my comfort in my affliction: for thy word hath quickened me" (Psalm 119:50).

v. "Unless thy law had been my delights, I should then have perished in mine affliction" (Psalm 119:92).

vi. Read Ephesians 4:29-32. Notice verse 31. It says, "Let all bitterness, and wrath, and anger, and clamour, and evil speaking, put away from you, with all malice."

vii. Hebrews 12:14-15 says, "Follow peace with all men, and holiness, without which no man shall see the Lord: Looking diligently lest any man fail of the grace of God; lest any root of bitterness springing up trouble you."

3. God never allows anything so that you will be bitter. Trials are for your good.
"*Difficulties are meant to rouse, not discourage. The human spirit is to grow strong by conflict.*"
William Ellery Channing

B. Three important attitudes to adopt during a trial are the following:

1. Humility

a. Luke 20:18 tells us to simply fall on the rock in submission and obedience instead of resisting. Resisting will cause deeper pain. It says, "Whosoever shall fall upon that stone shall be broken; but on whomsoever it shall fall, it will grind him to powder."

b. Ask for forgiveness. Let the trial be a time of cleansing.

   i. Psalm 25:17-18 says, "The troubles of my heart are enlarged: O bring thou me out of my distresses. Look upon mine affliction and my pain; and forgive all my sins."

   ii. I Peter 5:6-7 says, "Humble yourselves therefore under the mighty hand of God, that he may exalt you in due time: Casting all your care upon him; for he careth for you."

   iii. When Job had a humble spirit and prayed a prayer of repentance, God turned everything around for him. Job 42:6 says, "Wherefore I abhor myself, and repent in dust and ashes."

c. The good thing about a broken and submissive heart is that the Lord is near you. Read the following Scriptures:

   i. "The Lord is nigh unto them that are of a broken heart; and saveth such as be of a contrite spirit" (Psalm 34:18).

   ii. "He will regard the prayer of the destitute, and not despise their prayer" (Psalm 102:17).

iii. "He healeth the broken in heart, and bindeth up their wounds" (Psalm 147:3).

iv. To be able to bind up someone's wounds, you must be close enough to touch them.

2. Integrity

a. Psalm 17:3 says, "Thou hast proved mine heart; thou hast visited me in the night; thou hast tried me, and shalt find nothing; I am purposed that my mouth shall not transgress."

b. Psalm 32:2 says, "Blessed is the man unto whom the Lord imputeth not iniquity, and in whose spirit there is no guile."

c. Psalm 37:18 says, "The Lord knoweth the days of the upright: and their inheritance shall be for ever."

d. The upright will have trials and struggles, but the promise of the Lord is to deliver them out of all their troubles.

i. Read Psalm 37:23-25.

ii. Verse 23 says, "The steps of a good man are ordered by the Lord; and he delighteth in his way."

iii. Verse 24 says, "Though he fall, he shall not be utterly cast down: for the Lord upholdeth him with his hand."

iv. Verse 25 says, "I have been young, and now am old; yet have I not seen the righteous forsaken, nor his seed begging bread."

v. Psalm 37:39-40 says, "But the salvation of the righteous is of the Lord: he is their strength in the time of trouble. And the Lord shall help them, and deliver them: he shall deliver them from the wicked, and save them, because they trust in him."

e. Psalm 84:11 says, "For the Lord God is a sun and shield: the Lord will give grace and glory: no good thing will he withhold from them that walk uprightly."

3. Trust

a. Psalm 9:9-10 says, "The Lord will be a refuge for the oppressed, a refuge in times of trouble, and they that know thy name will put their trust in thee: for thou, Lord, hast not forsaken them that seek thee." The Lord will not forsake you.

b. The Lord will deliver you even from situations that are too big for you to handle. Read the following Scriptures:

i. "He delivered me from my strong enemy, and from them which hated me: for they were too strong for me" (Psalm 18:17).

ii. "For thou hast girded me with strength unto the battle: thou hast subdued under me those that rose up against me" (Psalm 18:39).

iii. "The Lord redeemeth the soul of his servants; and none of them that trust in him shall be desolate" (Psalm 34:22).

iv. “For he shall deliver the needy when he crieth, the poor also, and him that hath no helper” (Psalm 72:12).

c. Psalm 55:22 says, “Cast thy burden upon the Lord, and he shall sustain thee: he shall never suffer the righteous to be moved.”

d. Keep a fixed heart and do not waver.

i. “He shall not be afraid of evil tidings; his heart is fixed, trusting in the Lord” (Psalm 112:8).

ii. “O God, my heart is fixed; I will sing and give praise...” (Psalm 108:1).

iii. Hold on, my heart, in thy believing!
The steadfast only wear the crown;
He who, when stormy waves are heaving,
Parts with his anchor, shall go down;
But he whom Jesus holds thru all
Shall stand, though earth and heaven fall.

Hold out! There comes an end to sorrow;
Hope from the dust shall conquering rise;
The storm foretells a sunnier morrow;
The cross points on to Paradise.
The Father reigneth, cease all doubt;
Hold on, my heart, hold on, hold out.
Selected

C. Think on the Lord and past victories in Him, when you are in a trial. Hope in God always!

1. The Psalm of Asaph expresses how you feel when a trial is prolonged. Read the whole chapter but note the following verses specificially.

   a. "In the day of my trouble I sought the Lord: my sore ran in the night, and ceased not: my soul refused to be comforted" (Psalm 77:2).

   b. "I remembered God, and was troubled: I complained, and my spirit was overwhelmed. Selah" (Psalm 77:3).

   c. "Thou holdest mine eyes waking: I am so troubled that I cannot speak" (Psalm 77:4).

   d. "I have considered the days of old, the years of ancient times" (Psalm 77:5).

   e. "I will remember the words of the Lord: surely I will remember thy wonders of old. I will meditate also of all thy work, and talk of thy doings" (Psalm 77:11-12).

   f. This is how Asaph gained the victory. He meditated on the Lord and talked about the Lord and His greatness. He chose to magnify the Lord instead of his problem.

2. Psalm 43:5 says, "Why art thou cast down, O my soul? and why art thou disquieted within me? hope in God: for I shall yet praise him, who is the health of my countenance, and my God."

3. Do not let your mind dwell on the hurts. The anguish that you feel cannot be felt by the one that caused you pain. You are only hurting yourself when you nurse a grudge or hurt. An unknown author says it well in the following poem:

When some friend has proved untrue-betrayed your simple trust;
Used you for his selfish ends and trampled in the dust
The past, with all its memories and all its secret ties,
The light is blotted from the sky-for something in you dies.

Bless your false and faithless friend, just smile and pass along.
God must be the judge of it; He knows the right from wrong.
Life is short, don't waste the hours by brooding on the past.
His great laws are good and just; Truth conquers at the last.

Red and deep our wounds may be-but after all the pain.
God's own finger touches us and we are healed again.
With faith restored, and trust renewed-we look toward the stars.
The world will see the smiles we have-but God will see the scars.

D. Victory will come even when it looks dark if you keep trusting in Him. He will calm the storm.

1. Read Psalm 107:26-31.

a. *Verse 26* says, "They mount up to the heaven, they go down again to the depths: their soul is melted because of trouble."

b. `*Verse 27* says, "They reel to and fro, and stagger like a drunken man, and are at their wit's end."

c. *Verse 28* says, "Then they cry unto the Lord in their trouble, and he bringeth them out of their distresses."

d. *Verse 29* says, "He maketh the storm a calm, so that the waves thereof are still."

e. *Verse 30* says, "Then are they glad because they be quiet; so he bringeth them unto their desired haven."

f. *Verse 31* says, "O that men would praise the Lord for his goodness, and for his wonderful works to the children of men!"

2. Read Psalm 116:1-6.

a. *Verse 1* says, "I love the Lord, because he hath heard my voice and my supplication."

b. *Verse 2* says, "Because he hath inclined his ear unto me, therefore will I call upon him as long as I live."

c. *Verse 3* says, "The sorrows of death compassed me, and the pains of hell gat hold upon me: I found trouble and sorrow."

d. *Verse 4* says, "Then called I upon the name of the Lord; O Lord, I beseech thee, deliver my soul."

e. *Verses 5* says, "Gracious is the Lord, and righteous; yea, our God is merciful."

f. Verse 6 says, "The Lord preserveth the simple: I was brought low, and he helped me."

3. The Lord knows all about you and has a plan and a purpose for your life.

   a. Psalm 139:1-4 says, "O Lord thou hast searched me, and known me. Thou knowest my downsitting and mine uprising, thou understandest my thought afar off. Thou compassest my path and my lying down, and art acquainted with all my ways. For there is not a word in my tongue, but, lo, O Lord, thou knowest it altogether."

   b. I Peter 3:12 says, "For the eyes of the Lord are over the righteous, and his ears are open unto their prayers." He is listening and watching at all times.

   c. Psalms 37:18 says, "The Lord knoweth the days of the upright: and their inheritance shall be for ever."

   d. Romans 8:28 says, "And we know that all things work together for good to them that love God, to them who are the called according to his purpose."

E. A trial is the best thing that can happen to you. You should not seek after it, but when it comes, you will experience a time of growth, cleansing, self-examination, reflection, inspiration, and new beginnings.

   1. Your attitude will determine whether a trial is a blessing or a curse.

   2. *"Amid my list of blessings infinite, stands this the foremost, 'That my heart has bled.'"*
      Edward Young

3. The best things to do in a trial are the following:

a. Triumph

b. Rejoice

c. Increase

d. Abide

e. Learn

Lesson II Quiz

1. How can trials affect your life.

2. Give the two different attitudes you can choose and what they do for you.

3. What is the best way not to become offended?

4. Give three important attitudes to adopt in a trial. Give Bible references.

    a.

    b.

    c.

5. What will cause the victory to come?

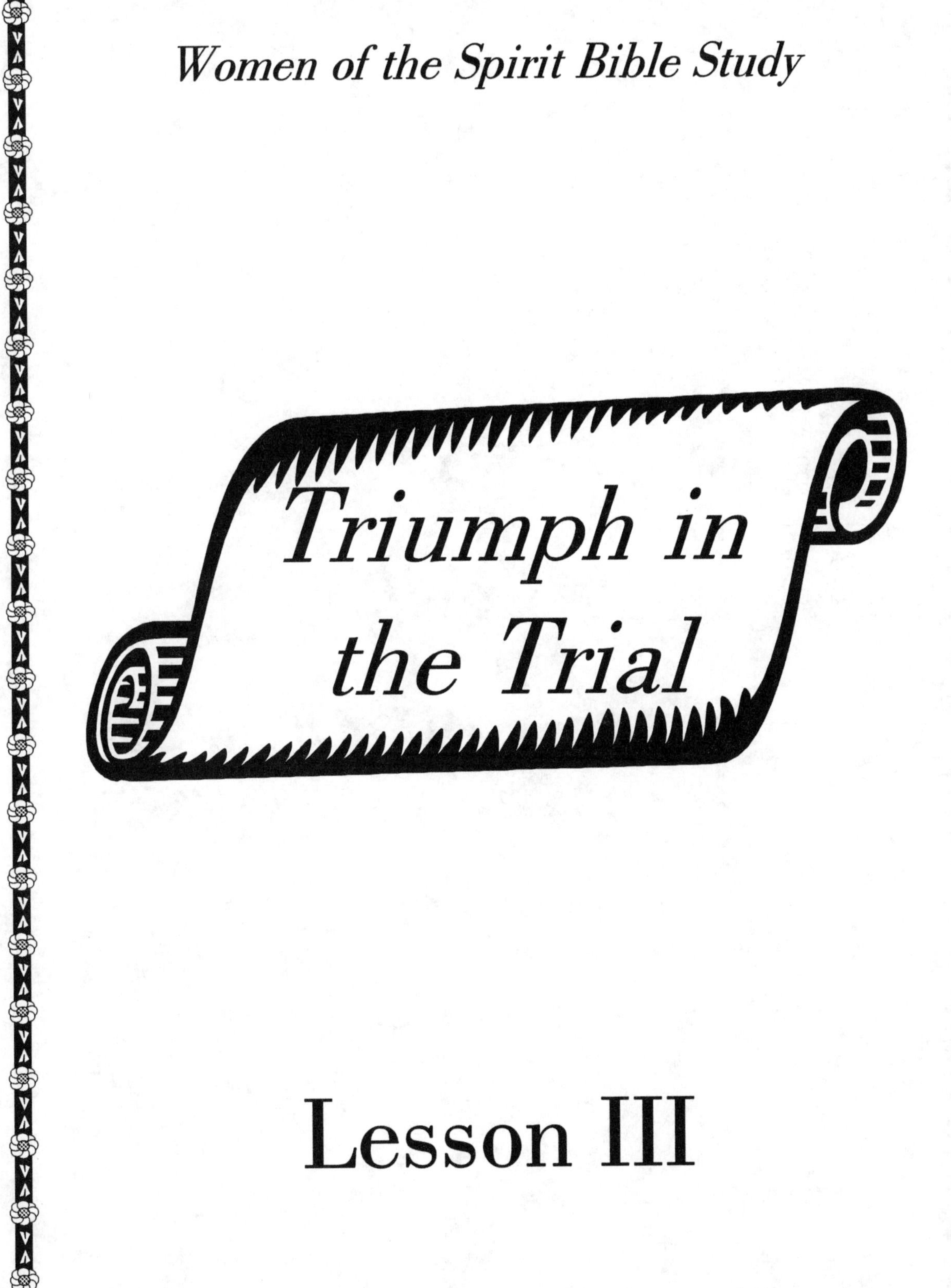
Women of the Spirit Bible Study
Triumph in the Trial
Lesson III

III. Triumph in the Trial

A. Transform your troubles into triumphs.

1. An unknown author wrote the following paragraph and poem that says it well: "The Christian way is to transform our troubles into triumph. Just as the oyster must put up with the irritable grain of sand and suffer the long process of spinning a gummy substance around the trouble spot to produce a pearl, our suffering can be transformed into a blessing. The liability can be changed into an asset. The adversity and disappointment can beget victory.

"*For every hill I've had to climb,*
For every stone that bruised my feet,
For all the blood and sweat and grime,
For blinding storms and burning heat,
My heart sings but a grateful song--
These were the things that made me strong.

For all the heartaches and the tears,
For all the anguish and the pain
For gloomy days and fruitless years,
And for the hopes that lived in vain,
I do give thanks, for now I know
These were the things that helped me grow!"

2. Triumph means to obtain victory, conquer, or overcome.

   a. Paul said in Romans 8:37, "Who shall separate us from the love of Christ? shall tribulation, or distress...Nay, in all these things we are more than conquerors through him that loved us."

   b. In the letters to the seven churches in the book of Revelation, each ended with the phrase, *He that overcometh.* The important thing for each church was that they would overcome all the trials, tribulations, and temptations that came to them. The Bible established that every person, family, and church will go through some testing. The end result is what matters the most.

      i. *Ephesus* "To him that **overcometh** will I give to eat of the tree of life which is in the midst of the paradise of God" (Revelation 2:7).

      ii. *Smyrna* "He that **overcometh** shall not be hurt of the second death" (Revelation 2:11).

      iii. *Pergamos* "To him that **overcometh** will I give to eat of the hidden manna" (Revelation 2:17).

      iv. *Thyatira* "He that overcometh, and keepeth my words unto the end, to him will I give power over the nations" (Revelation 2:26).

      v. *Sardis* "He that overcometh, the same shall be clothed in white raiment" (Revelation 3:5).

vi. *Philadelphia* "He that **overcometh**...I will write upon him my new name" (Revelation 3:12).

vii. *Laodicea* "To him that **overcometh** will I grant to sit with me in my throne" (Revelation 3:21).

c. Revelation 21:7 says, "He that overcometh shall inherit all things; and I will be his God, and he shall be my son."

d. Every trial you walk through is the opportunity for another victory.

e. *"Christianity is a battle, not a dream."*
Wendell Phillips

B. Defeat is not final. Trials and setbacks are temporary. The victory will come, for the Lord is working something good out for you.

1. Edwin Markham writes:
"Defeat may serve as well as victory
To shake the soul and let the glory out.
When the great oak is straining in the wind,
The boughs drink in new beauty, and the trunk
Sends down a deeper root on the windward side.
Only the soul that knows the mighty grief
Can know the mighty rapture. Sorrows come
To stretch our spaces in the heart for joy."

2. II Corinthians 4:17 says, "For our light affliction, which is but for a moment, worketh for us a far more exceeding and eternal weight of glory."

3. When Joseph went through extreme heartbreak, rejection and despair, it looked like utter defeat. But God had a greater plan that any human eye could see.

    a. Genesis 50:20 says, "But as for you, ye thought evil against me; but God meant it unto good, to bring to pass, as it is this day, to save much people alive."

    b. Psalm 105:17-19 says, "He (God) sent a man before them, even Joseph, who was sold for a servant: Whose feet they hurt with fetters: he was laid in iron: Until the time that his word came: the word of the Lord tried him."

    c. The Lord tried Joseph. He was preparing him for greater things. As Joseph was laid in iron, the iron entered into his very soul, strengthening him. The years of hurt were not defeat, but they served as a forerunner of great blessing.

C. Be of good courage. Things will get better if you stay close to Jesus.

1. The Lord spoke to Joshua after the death of Moses and said, "Have not I commanded thee? Be strong and of a good courage; be not afraid, neither be thou dismayed: for the Lord thy God is with thee whithersoever thou goest" (Joshua 1:9).

2. Courage means that quality of mind and spirit which enables one to meet danger and difficulties with firmness and valor. It keeps one going in spite of opposition, with determination and purpose.

3. Karle Wilson Baker writes the following poem:
"Courage is armor
A blind man wears;
The callused scar
Of outlived despairs;
Courage is Fear
That has said its prayers."

4. Moses spoke his last counsels to the people of Israel in Deuteronomy 31:6. It says, "Be strong and of a good courage, fear not, nor be afraid of them: for the Lord thy God, he it is that doth go with thee; he will not fail thee, nor forsake thee."

5. Psalm 27:14 says, "Wait on the Lord: be of good courage, and he shall strengthen thine heart; wait, I say, on the Lord."

6. "When you get into a tight place and everything goes against you, till it seems as though you could not hold on a minute longer, never give up then, for that is just the place and time that the tide will turn." Harriet Beecher Stowe

7. The Lord desires His children to speak courage to one another.

   a. "They helped every one his neighbour; and every one said to his brother, Be of good courage" (Isaiah 41:6).

   b. "Then they that feared the Lord spake often one to another; and the Lord hearkened, and heard it, and a book of remembrance was written before him for them that feared the Lord, and that thought upon his name. And they shall be mine, saith the Lord of hosts, in that day when I make up my jewels" (Malachi 3:16-17).

c. Joshua spoke the same message to the same people which Moses had spoken years before. "And Joshua said unto them, Fear not, nor be dismayed, be strong and of good courage: for thus shall the Lord do to all your enemies against whom ye fight."

8. Edgar A. Guest gives us the following poem:

"This is courage: to remain
Brave and patient under pain;
Cool and calm and firm to stay
In the presence of dismay;
Not to flinch when foes attack
Even though you're beaten back;
Still to cling to what is right,
When the wrong possesses might.

This is courage: to be true
To the best men see in you;
To remember, tempest-tossed,
Not to whimper, "All is lost!"
But to battle to the end
While you still have strength to spend;
Not to cry that hope is gone
While you've life to carry on.

This is courage; to endure
Hurt and loss you cannot cure;
Patiently and undismayed,
Facing life still unafraid;
Glad to live and glad to take
Bravely for your children's sake,
Burdens they would have to bear
If you fled and ceased to care."

9. Paul had the ability to take courage. Acts 28:15 says, "And from thence, when the brethren heard of us, they came to meet us as far as Appii forum, and The three taverns: whom when Paul saw, he thanked God, and took courage."

D. The *Lord* will cause you to triumph in the time of trial and trouble.

1. II Corinthians 2:14 says, "Now thanks be unto God, which always causeth us to triumph in Christ."

2. Psalm 46:1 says, "God is our refuge and strength, a very present help in trouble."

3. Pray this poem during the time of your trial so you can triumph.
God, make me brave for life; oh, braver than this.
Let me straighten after pain, as a tree straightens after the rain,
Shining and lovely again.
God make me brave for life; much braver than this.
As the blown grass lifts, let me rise
From sorrow with quiet eyes,
Knowing Thy way is wise.
God, make me brave, life brings
Such blinding things.
Help me to keep my sight;
Help me to see aright
That out of dark comes light.
Author unknown

4. I Corinthians 15:57 says, "But thanks be to God, which giveth us the victory through our Lord Jesus Christ."

5. "For those who will fight bravely and not yield, there is triumphant victory over all the dark things of life."
James Allen

6. “St. Ambrose says that a Christian wife was on a journey with her heathen husband, when a terrific thunder-storm arose, which overwhelmed the man with terror. His wife asked the cause. He replied, ‘Are you not afraid?’ She answered, ‘No, not at all: for I know that it is the voice of my heavenly Father; and shall a child be afraid of a father's voice?’
The husband saw that his wife had what he had not; and this led him to the adoption of Christianity.”

Foster

Lesson III Quiz

1. How can you transform your troubles into triumph?

2. What does triumph mean?

3. What was the same message given to the seven churches?

4. Explain what courage is and give four biblical references referring to it.

   a.

   b.

   c.

   d.

   e.

Women of the Spirit Bible Study

Lesson IV

IV. Rejoice in the Trial

A. The following are interesting facts concerning trials and rejoicing.

1. The word *trials* is not mentioned in the Bible.
   The word *trial* is only mentioned six times.
   The word *temptation* is mentioned 22 times; whereas the word *temptations* is mentioned only eight.

2. On the other hand, the word *rejoice* is mentioned 192 times. The word *joy* is mentioned 165 times.

3. The words most frequently used with the words *trial* and *temptation* are joy or rejoice.

   a. "How that in a great *trial* of affliction the abundance of their *joy*...abounded" (II Corinthians 8:2).

   b. "Beloved, think it not strange concerning the fiery *trial* which is to try you...But *rejoice*" (I Peter 4:12-13).

c. "My brethren, count it all *joy* when ye fall into divers *temptations*" (James 1:2).

d. "...I am filled with comfort, I am exceeding *joyful* in all our *tribulation*" (II Corinthians 7:4).

e. "Wherein ye greatly *rejoice*, though now for a season, if need be, ye are in heaviness through manifold *temptations*" (I Peter 1:6).

4. This does not make sense in terms of human wisdom, but it is God's way to victory.

5. Webster's definitions are as following:

a. Joy means gladness or delight; to rejoice.

b. Rejoice means to *feel* joy or great delight.

6. Matthew Henry says joy is a constant delight in God.

D. The Bible teaches us to rejoice in the Lord when we are going through a trial or a time of suffering.

1. Read Habakkuk 3:17-18.

a. Verse 17 says, "Although the fig tree shall not blossom, neither shall fruit be in the vines; the labour of the olive shall fail, and the fields shall yield no meat; the flock shall be cut off from the fold, and there shall be no herd in the stalls."

b. Verse 18 says, "Yet [in spite of everything being bad] I will rejoice in the Lord, I will joy in the God of my salvation."

2. Psalm 5:11 says, "But let all those that put their trust in thee rejoice: let them ever shout for joy, because thou defendest them: let them also that love thy name be joyful in thee."

   a. Why would they need to be defended if they were not in trouble? The use of the word "defendest" implies that they were in a battle.

   b. Why would they need to trust if all was well?

3. Matthew 5:11-12 says, "Blessed are ye, when men shall revile you, and persecute you, and shall say all manner of evil against you falsely, for my sake. Rejoice, and be exceeding glad: for great is your reward in heaven: for so persecuted they the prophets which were before you."

4. Colossians 1:24 says, "Who now rejoice in my sufferings for you, and fill up that which is behind of the afflictions of Christ in my flesh, for his body's sake, which is the church."

5. I Peter 4:12-13 says, "Beloved, think it not strange concerning the fiery trial which is to try you, as though some strange thing happened unto you. But rejoice, inasmuch as ye are partakers of Christ's sufferings; that, when his glory shall be revealed, ye may be glad also with exceeding joy."

   a. Verse 12 says, "Beloved, think it not strange concerning the fiery trial which is to try you."

   b. Other translations provide further meanings:

      i. "*Do not be bewildered.*"
      New English Bible

ii. "*Do not be astonished.*"
The Twentieth Century New Testament

iii. "*that a test of fire is being applied to you.*"
Edgar J. Goodspeed

iv. "*at the fiery test taking place among you to prove you.*"
John Broadus

v. "*at the fiery ordeal coming among you to put you to the test.*"
Richard Francis Weymouth

6. Paul describes the example of Macedonia in II Corinthians 8:2. "How that in a *great trial of affliction the abundance of their joy* and their deep poverty abounded unto the riches of their liberality."

7. I Thessalonians 1:6 says, "And ye became followers of us, and of the Lord, having received the word in much affliction, with joy of the Holy Ghost." The Holy Ghost, which is the presence of God in you, gives you joy.

   a. Romans 14:17 says, "For the kingdom of God is not meat and drink; but righteousness and peace, and joy in the Holy Ghost."

   b. Romans 15:13 says, "Now the God of hope fill you with all joy and peace in believing, that ye may abound in hope, through the power of the Holy Ghost." Do not under rate the Holy Ghost, but reverence and respect it and let the fullness of it fill your mind, soul, and spirit.

8. David said in Psalm 31:7, "I will be glad and rejoice in thy mercy: for thou hast considered my trouble; thou hast known my soul in adversities."

9. The above trials, sufferings, and afflictions are all related to those who were living uprightly. When trials are caused by sin, there must be repentance before rejoicing. When sickness comes, there must be a prayer of faith made according to James 5:13-16 which says, "Is any among you afflicted? let him pray. Is any merry? let him sing psalms. Is any sick among you? let him call for the elders of the church; and let them pray over him, anointing him with oil in the name of the Lord: And the prayer of faith shall save the sick, and the Lord shall raise him up: and if he have committed sins, they shall be forgiven him. Confess your faults one to another, and pray one for another, that ye may be healed. The effectual fervent prayer of a righteous man availeth much." Prayer is very much a part of every aspect of any one who needs help. There is the prayer of faith and the prayer of repentance noted here. There must be forgiveness before healing can come. Humility is always God's way.

10. Trials come from different sources. The **devil** will tempt you as he did Jesus in Matthew 4. The **devil** will cause you trouble as he did in Job 1-2. The **Lord** will try you as he did Abraham in Genesis 22:1. **Your own actions** can bring disastrous trials, such as Jonah in Jonah 1-4. **People** around you can cause disturbances, and trouble you as they did for Daniel in Daniel 6. Lastly, **life is imperfect** because of the sin in the garden. When sin entered the human race because of Adam and Eve's disobedience, trials, temptations, tears, and sorrow entered with it. Matthew 5:45 says, "For he maketh his sun to rise on the evil and on the good, and sendeth rain on the just and on the unjust." You cannot escape trials, but how you handle them will make a difference.

11. You have a choice when life in general closes in on you. You can either feel sorry for yourself and nurse your wounds, or you can focus on the Lord and delight in His promises. The following story shared by Donald Grey Barnhouse about a woman who lived in New York says it well. "One very rainy night, a little over a year ago, I locked my store and started home. There was a pouring, drenching, chilling rain and high wind. An umbrella was useless. The cars were late, and I waited on the corner for three quarters of an hour. I was soaked to the skin, and chilled to the bone. Then I had to ride in two cold cars. When I reached home there was no dry clothing laid out for me, there was no warm supper, the fires were banked and the house was cold. Now the Lord has been good to me. He has blessed me with a happy disposition--the 'blue devils' do not trouble me often. But they were there that night. I thought: I will feed my kitten. I will not bother with any supper. I will go right to bed and cry it out.

I began to remove my soaked clothing, and as I did, the Lord brought these words to my mind:
There is never a day so dreary,
There is never a night so long,
But the soul that is trusting Jesus
Will somewhere, somehow find a song.

E. Joy does not mean that trouble is absent, it is simply the abiding presence of the Lord.

1. Psalm 16:11 says, "Thou wilt shew me the path of life; in thy presence is fulness of joy: at thy right hand there are pleasures for evermore."

2. Psalm 43:4 says, "Then will I go unto the altar of God, unto God my exceeding joy."

3. Principal Rainy used a good metaphor about a Christian's joy. "Joy," he said, "is the flag which is flown from the castle of the heart when the King is in residence there."

F. God intended you to finish your course with joy, not defeat!

1. Jude 1:24 says, "Now unto him that is able to keep you from falling, and to present you faultless before the presence of his glory with exceeding joy."

2. Paul said in Acts 20:24, "But none of these things move me, neither count I my life dear unto myself, so that I might finish my course with joy."

3. Jesus did not accept *defeat*, but looked ahead to the victory.

a. Matthew 26:37-38 says, "And he took with him Peter and the two sons of Zebedee, and began to be sorrowful and very heavy. Then saith he unto them, My soul is exceeding sorrowful, even unto death."

b. But He finished with joy. Hebrews 12:2 says, "Looking unto Jesus the author and finisher of our faith; who for the *joy* that was set before him *endured* the cross."

c. Because Jesus wept and wrought a great victory, we can rejoice!

G. The joy of the Lord is a testimony of Christ's power in the life of a believer.

1. Many years ago when missionary Adoniram Judson was home on furlough, he passed through the city of Stonington, Connecticut. A young boy playing about the wharves at the time of Judson's arrival was struck by the man's appearance. Never before had he seen such a light on any human face. He ran up the street to a minister to

ask if he knew who the stranger was. The minister hurried back with him, but became so absorbed in conversation with Judson that he forgot all about the impatient youngster standing near him.

Many years afterward that boy, who could never get away from the influence of that wonderful face, became the famous preacher Henry Clay Trumbell. In a book of memoirs he penned a chapter entitled: "What a Boy Saw in the Face of Adoniram Judson." That lighted countenance had changed his life.

2. My question to Christian women is this: "What do the children, the unbelievers, or the family see in your face?"

3. Christians go through some of the same trials as unbelievers, but they face them differently because they have hope.

    a. In dealing with death Paul says in I Thessalonians 4:13, "Ye sorrow not, even as others which have no hope."

    b. Read Philippians 1:12-30. Notice especially verses 13 and 18. Even in his bonds Paul rejoiced.

        i. Verse 13 says, "So that my bonds in Christ are manifest in all the palace, and in all other places."

        ii. Verse 18 says, "What then? notwithstanding, every way, whether in pretence, or in truth, Christ is preached: and I therein do rejoice, yea, and will rejoice."

4. Read Psalm 126:2-6. Note especially verse 2. "Then was our mouth filled with laughter, and our tongue with singing: then said they among the heathen, The Lord hath done great things for them."

H. A thankful spirit should accompany every trial. This gives strength to rejoice.

1. I Thessalonians 5:18 says, "In every thing give thanks; for this is the will of God in Christ Jesus concerning you." The will of God is to give thanks in every trial.

2. Ephesians 5:20 says, "Giving thanks always for all things unto God and the Father in the name of our Lord Jesus Christ." Giving thanks forever for everything is what is required for the believer.

3. Colossians 3:17 says, "And whatsoever ye do in word or deed, do all in the name of the Lord Jesus, giving thanks to God and the Father by him."

4. David couples rejoicing and a person's need together. Psalm 70:4-5 says, "Let all those that seek thee rejoice and be glad in thee: and let such as love thy salvation say continually, Let God be magnified. But I am poor and needy: make haste unto me O God: thou art my help and my deliverer; O Lord, make no tarrying."

5. Worshipping and magnifying God in the trial is necessary to have victory. Psalm 70:4-5 says, "Let all those that seek thee rejoice and be glad in thee; and let such as love thy salvation say continually, Let God be magnified. But I am poor and needy: make haste unto me, O God; thou art my help and my deliver; O Lord, make no tarrying."

5. Nehemiah 8:10 says, "...for the joy of the Lord is your strength."

I. Happiness is dependent upon things; joy is dependent upon God.

1. Carlton Myers writes the following. "Happiness and joy are not the same. Happiness is determined by the happenings, events, and circumstances of life. Joy is

determined by the fulness of the Holy Spirit in our lives. So it is possible to be joyful even though you are unhappy. The fulness of the Holy spirit in us is determined by how much we have surrendered our wills to God. It is also determined by how much of God's word is in us.

"Happiness is not something you find by searching for it. It is a by-product of losing yourself in serving God and others. The same is true of joy. You cannot work it up. It is a supernatural result of God's spirit."

2. A preacher was once crossing the Atlantic and a young man, a fellow-passenger, having an intense desire for an interview with him, went to his cabin door and knocked gently. As no answer was received he quietly opened the door, to find the great saint of God prostrate upon the floor, his hands raised to heaven and his lips moving in prayer. These were the words which he heard: "O Lord Jesus, Thou hast filled my life with peace and gladness. To look into Thy face is earth's most exquisite joy."

3. Cyprian wrote of the time of the early Christians: "This is a cheerful world as I see it from my garden, under the shadow of my vines. But if I could ascend some high mountain and look out over the wide lands, you know very well what I would see--brigands on the highways; pirates on the seas; armies fighting, cities burning; in the amphi-theatres men murdered to please applauding crowds; selfishness and cruelty, misery and despair under all roofs. It is a bad world.

"But I have discovered in the midst of it a quiet and holy people who have learned a great secret. They have found a joy which is a thousand times better than any of the pleasures of our sinful life. They are despised and persecuted, but they care not. They are masters of their own souls. They have overcome the world. These people, Donatus, are the Christians--and I am one of them."

Quiz for Lesson IV

1. How many times are the words "trial" and "trials" mentioned in the Bible?

2. Give definitions of joy and rejoice.

   a.

   b.

3. Give essence and explain Habakkuk 3:17-18 and I Peter 4:12-13.

   a.

   b.

4. Trials come from what sources?

   a.

   b.

   c.

   d.

5. Give biblical examples of those who rejoiced in the trial.

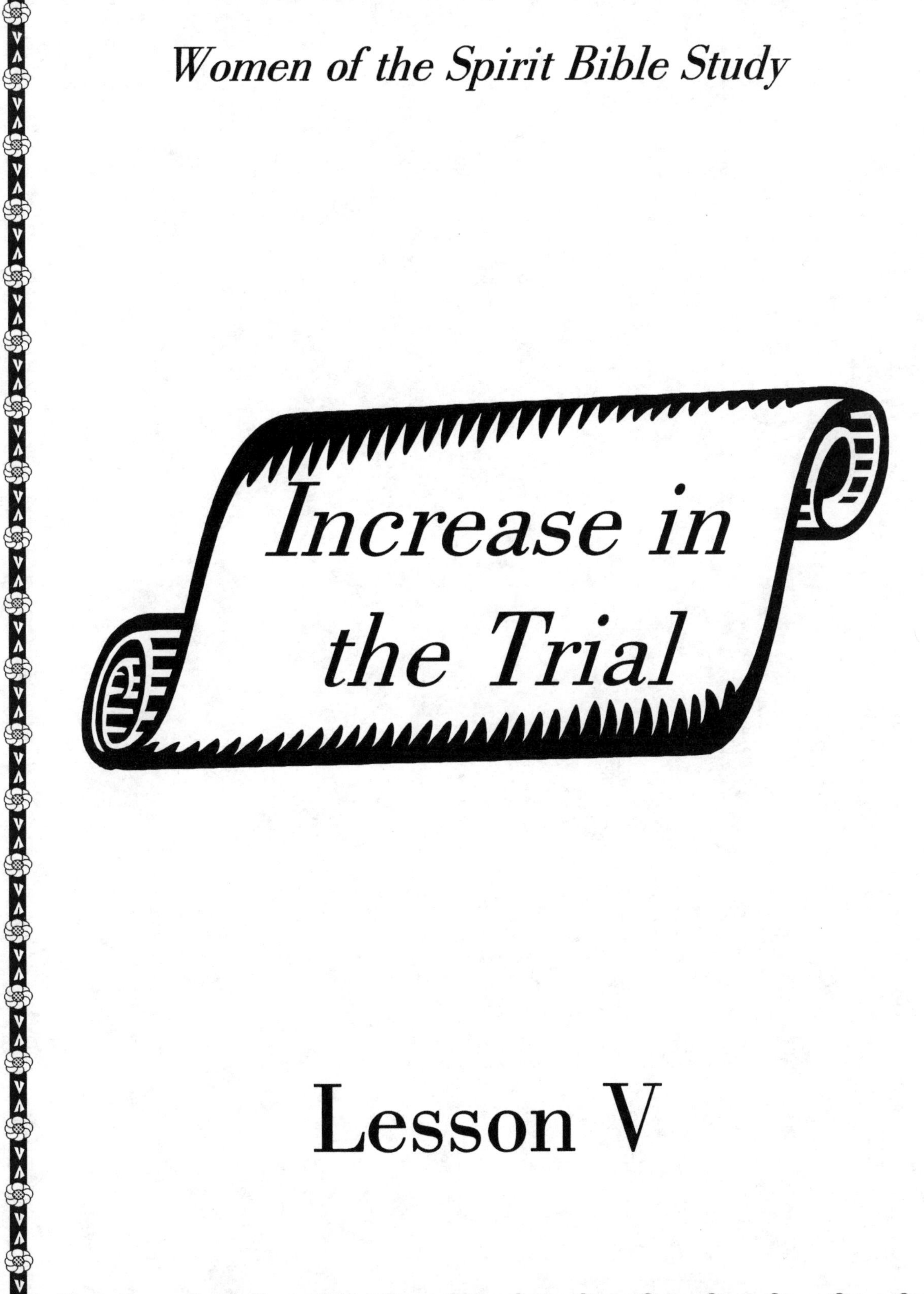
Women of the Spirit Bible Study
Increase in the Trial
Lesson V

V. Increase in the Trial

A. Trials are supposed to increase you in the Lord. They are not to discourage; they are to heal inner conflicts and perfect you.

1. Psalm 115:13-14 says, "He will bless them that fear the Lord, both small and great. The Lord shall increase you more and more, you and your children."

2. In nature many times seeds or plants are increased by death or dividing.

a. John 12:24 says, "Except a corn of wheat fall into the ground and die, it abideth alone: but if it die, it bringeth forth much fruit."

b. The grape grower knows that in order for the most lucious fruit to come forth, he must cut back and prune the vine.

c. Paul R. Van Gorden writes, "Dr. Issac Page, told afterward of traveling one day through the fruit regions in the West. There he saw how the growers pruned their trees in order to get a maximum yield. He noticed in particular an apricot orchard where the owner was busy cutting back the branches. To one who knew nothing about raising fruit, this activity looked like a needle work of mutilation. But the man doing the job knew exactly what was needed to get the best results.

"Dr. Page learned that the next spring the same trees were pruned again, though not so severely. When the fruit was fully formed, the farmer carefully thinned out the crop. Then by autumn harvest time, the trees were laden with delicious apricots. The pruning knife of the husbandman had accomplished its intended purpose."

3. In the parable of the sower Jesus gave an example of four different groups of people, but only one of them increased. It was how the Word was received during a trial that affected their increase or decrease. Read Matthew 13:19-23; Luke 8:5-15; and Mark 7:3-20. Note specifically Mark 4:15-20.

   a. Verse 15 says, "And these are they by the way side, where the word is sown; but when they have heard, Satan cometh immediately, and taketh away the word that was sown in their hearts."

   b. Verses 16-17 says, "And these are they likewise which are sown on stony ground; who, when they have heard the word, immediately receive it with gladness. And have no root in themselves, and so endure but for a time: afterward, when affliction or persecution ariseth for the word's sake, immediately they are offended."

c. Verses 18-19 says, "And these are they which are sown among thorns; such as hear the word, And the cares of this world, and the deceitfulness of richness, and the lusts of other things entering in, choke the word, and it becometh unfruitful."

d. Verse 20 says, "And these are they which are sown on good ground; such as hear the word, and receive it, and bring forth fruit, some thirtyfold, some sixty, and some an hundred."

4. The poem, "Friendly Obstacles" expresses how the difficulties of life are actually the seedbed for increase.
For every hill I've had to climb,
For every stone that bruised my feet,
For all the blood and sweat and grime,
For blinding storms and burning heat,
My heart sings but a grateful song--
These were the things that made me strong.

For all the heartaches and the tears,
For all the anguish and the pain,
For gloomy days and fruitless years,
And for the hopes that lived in vain,
I do give thanks, for now I know
These were the things that helped me grow!

'Tis not the softer things of life
Which stimulate man's will to strive;
But bleak adversity and strife
Do more to keep man's will alive.
O'er rose-strewn paths the weaklings creep,
But brave hearts dare to climb the steep.

B. The righteous shall flourish.

1. Psalm 92:12-13 says, "The righteous shall flourish like the palm tree: he shall grow like a cedar in Lebanon. Those that be planted in the house of the Lord shall flourish in the courts of our God."

2. Flourish means to blossom, to grow luxuriantly, thrive, increase in honor, or to reach the climax of development or influence.

3. The trunk of the palm tree is very light, but exceedingly flexible and strong. It sways to and fro in the wind with inexpressible gracefulness, but seldom breaks, even in the fiercest gales. The tall, slender, flexible trunk springs from an immense tuber, a little below the surface of the ground. From the lower surface of this tuber descend cord-like white roots, which extend downward six to eight feet or more. Its foliage is continually green and it gives a wealth of delicious fruit. (The righteous are as the palm tree, for they are able to bend with the trial and because of their strong root system they are not destroyed. They are rooted in Christ which gives them the strength to be graceful under pressure.)

   a. Colossians 2:6 says, "As ye have therefore received Christ Jesus the Lord, so walk ye in him:"

   b. Colosians 2:7 says, "Rooted and built up in him, and stablished in the faith."

4. The poem, "*Cedar Christians,*" should be our daily prayer.

Jesus, help me to be for Thee,
Just like a big, strong cedar tree;
When all the other trees are bare,
The cedar stands so green and fair,

The wind and storm the ice and cold
Make it more beauty to unfold.
So I would stand in trial and test,
Just trusting You to do what's best,
Though others fail, Lord, keep Thou me!
May I a cedar Christian Be."

Author unknown

C. The Lord desires for you to increase in the following virtures:

1. Love

a. "And the Lord make you to increase and abound in love one toward another, and toward all men, even as we do toward you" (I Thessalonians 3:12).

b. "Beloved, let us love one another: for love is of God; and every one that loveth is born of God, and knoweth God" (I John 4:7).

2. Joy

a. "The meek also shall increase their joy in the Lord" (Isaiah 29:19).

b. "These things have I spoken unto you, that my joy might remain in you, and that your joy might be full" (John 15:11).

3. Knowledge of God

a. "That ye might walk worthy of the Lord unto all pleasing, being fruitful in every good work, and increasing in the knowledge of God" (Colossians 1:10).

b. "But grow in grace, and in the knowledge of our Lord and Saviour Jesus Christ" (II Peter 3:18).

4. Faith

   a. "We are bound to thank God always for you, brethren, as it is meet, because that your faith groweth exceedingly, and the charity of every one of you all toward each other aboundeth" (II Thessalonians 1:3).

   b. "That your faith should not stand in the wisdom of men, but in the power of God" (I Corinthians 2:5). To His kingdom, there is no end. It is continual increase from glory to glory.

5. Patience

   a. Read II Peter 1:5-8.

      i. Verse 5 says, "And beside this, giving all diligence, **add** to your faith virtue; and to virtue knowledge."

      ii. Verse 6 says, "And to knowledge temperance; and to temperance patience; and to patience godliness."

      iii. Verse 7 says, "And to godliness brotherly kindness; and to brotherly kindness charity."

      iv. Verse 8 says, "For if these things be in you, and **abound**, they make you that ye shall neither be barren nor unfruitful in the knowledge of our Lord Jesus Christ."

   b. "But that on the good ground are they, which in an honest and good heart, having heard the word, keep it, and bring forth fruit with patience" (Luke 8:15).

D. God's investment program vs. the devil's.

1. All of the devil's schemes and enticements eventually subtract from you. There is never an abounding in good or an increase; whereas God may sometimes subtract, but He always gives increase in the life of the believer. Not only does He increase in this life, but the increase in the hereafter is unsearchable riches.

2. "But as it is written, Eye hath not seen, nor ear heard, neither have entered into the heart of man, the things which God hath prepared for them that love him" (I Corinthians 2:9).

3. "That he would grant you, according to the riches of his glory, to be strengthened with might by his Spirit in the inner man. Now unto him that is able to do exceeding abundantly above all that we ask of think, according to the power that worketh in us" (Ephesians 3:16 & 20).

4. It may look like God does not know what He is doing but He does. The poem, *The Loom of Time*, says it well.

Man's life is laid in the loom of time
To a pattern he does not see,
While the weavers work and the shuttles fly
Till the dawn of eternity.

Some shuttles are filled with silver threads
And some with threads of gold,
While often but the darker hues
Are all that they may hold.

But the weaver watches with skillful eye
Each shuttle fly to and fro,
And sees the pattern so deftly wrought
As the loom moves sure and slow.

God surely planned the patterns
Each thread, the dark and fair,
Is chosen by His master skill
And placed in the web with care.

He only knows its beauty,
And guides the shuttles which hold
The threads so unattractive,
As well as the threads of gold.

Not till each loom is silent,
And the shuttles cease to fly,
Shall God reveal the pattern
And explain the reason why

The dark threads were as needful
In the weaver's skillful hand
As the threads of gold and silver
For the pattern which He planned.
Author unknown

E. God's ways are not our ways. Decreasing is the way to increase.

1. John 3:30 says, "He must increase, but I must decrease."

2. Jesus said in Luke 9:24, "For whosoever will save his life shall lose it: but whosoever will lose his life for my sake, the same shall save it."

3. Paul said, "When I am weak, then am I strong" (II Corinthians 12:10).

4. As your self will, arrogance, and carnal flesh decreases because of suffering, trials, and tears, Christ can abound in you. He only dwells with the humble.

5. II Corinthians 1:5 says, "For as the sufferings of Christ abound in us, so our consolation also aboundeth by Christ."

6. The woman who is forced to her knees can become the greatest Christian ever. W. Hayden Ambrose says it like this. "A maker of violins searched all his life for wood that would serve for making violins with a certain beautiful and haunting resonance. At last he succeeded when he came into possession of wood gathered from the timberline, the last stand of the trees of the Rockies, 12,000 feet above sea level. Up there where the winds blow so fiercely and steadily that the bark to windward has no chance to grow, where the branches all point one way, and where a tree must stay on its knees all through its life, that is where the world's most resonant wood for violins is born and lives and dies."

F. God's retirement program is glory, gold, and generous gifts forevermore. Satan's retirement program is hell, fire, gnashing of teeth, and misery forevermore.

1. Revelation 21:7-8 says, "He that overcometh shall inherit all things; and I will be his God, and he shall be my son. But the fearful, and unbelieving and the abominable, and murderers, and whoremongers, and sorcerers, and idolaters, and all liars, shall have their part in the lake which burneth with fire and brimstone."

2. God's promises are exquisite. "And God shall wipe away all tears from their eyes; and there shall be no more death, neither sorrow, nor crying, neither shall there be any more pain: for the former things are passed away" (Revelation 21:4).

3. The devil's home is pure hell. "And the devil that deceived them was cast into the lake of fire and brimstone, where the beast and the false prophet are, and shall be tormented day and night for ever and ever. And whosoever was not found written in the book of life was cast into the lake of fire" (Revelation 20:10 & 15).

G. Devil means evil; God means good. Add the letter *d* to evil and you have devil. Subract the letter *o* from good and you have God.

1. John 10:10 says, "The thief cometh not, but for to steal, and to kill, and to destroy: I am come that they might have life, and that they might have it more abundantly."

2. Satan stole from Job, but God increased him.

   a. "So went Satan forth from the presence of the Lord, and smote Job with sore boils from the sole of his foot unto his crown" (Job 2:7). Before this, Satan had taken away all of his children, oxen, sheep, servants, and camels.

   b. "So the Lord blessed the latter end of Job more than his beginning: for he had fourteen thousand sheep, and six thousand camels, and a thousand yoke of oxen, and a thousand she asses. He had also seven sons and three daughters" (Job 42:12-13).

3. Job's attitude at the beginning of his trial should be the attitude of every woman during her trials and losses. When Job learned he had lost everything he did several things. "Then Job arose, and rent his mantle, and shaved his head, and fell down upon the ground, and worshipped. And said, Naked came I out of my mother's womb, and naked shall I return thither: the Lord gave, and the Lord hath taken away; blessed be the name of the Lord. In all this Job sinned not, nor charged God foolishly" (Job 1:20-22).

4. After he lost everything he worshipped. He worshipped before God increased him.

Quiz for Lesson V

1. Trials are to ______________ you in the Lord.

2. In nature what is necessary for growth?

3. Give four soils and explain how they relate to mankind.

    a.

    b.

    c.

    d.

4. Explain Psalm 92:12-12.

    a.

    b.

5. Give five virtues a woman should increase in.

    a.

    b.

    c.

    d.

    e.

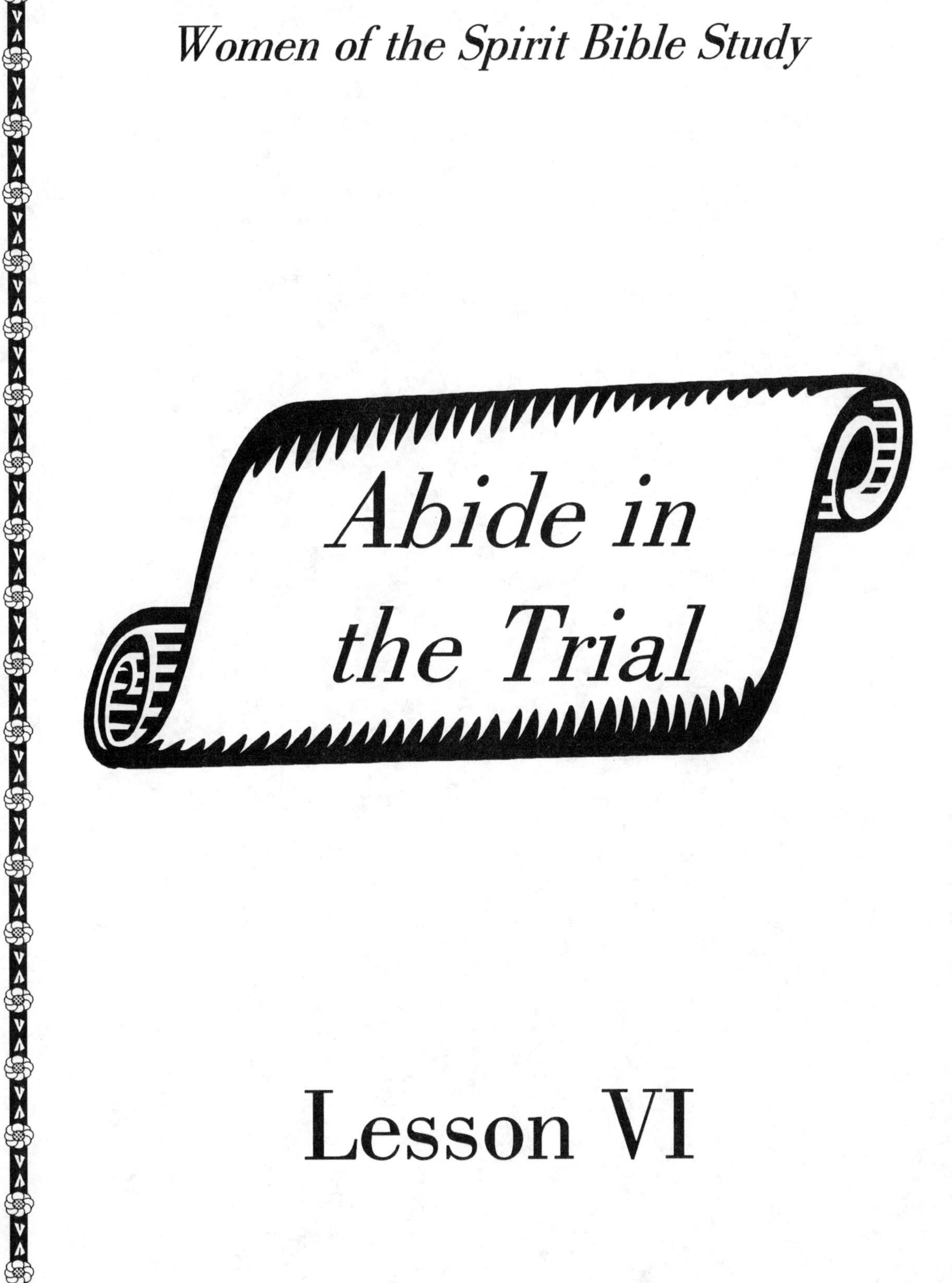
Women of the Spirit Bible Study
Abide in the Trial
Lesson VI

VI. Abide in the Trial

A. The safest place in a trial is in the arms of the Lord.

1. Read Psalm 91:1-2.

a. Verse 1 says, "He that dwelleth in the secret place of the most High shall abide under the shadow of the Almighty."

b. Verse 2 says, "I will say of the Lord, He is my refuge and my fortress: my God; in him will I trust."

c. The Lord is your refuge.

d. Mrs. Charles Cowman relates the following story. "One night during a terrific storm a man walked along the shore of the sea. The clouds hung low overhead. The wind howled. Thunders roared. Lightning flashed and the rain poured down in torrents. The man pulled his overcoat closer around him, bent his body to the wind and hurried home. A little bird lost in the storm sought shelter under his coat; he took it in his hand, carried it home, placed it in a warm cage. The next morning after the storm had subsided, and the clouds had cleared away, he took the little bird to the door. It paused on his hand for a moment; then lifting its tiny wings, it hurried back to its forest home. Then it was that Charles Wesley caught the vision, and going back to his room he wrote the words to a song that is loved around the world today and will live on in time:"

Jesus, Lover of my soul
Let me to thy bosom fly,
While the nearer waters roll,
While the tempest still is high:

Hide me, O my Saviour, hide,
Till the storm of life be past;
Safe into the haven guide,
O receive my soul at last!

Other refuge have I none,
Hangs my helpless soul on thee;
Leave, ah! leave me not alone,
Still support and comfort me.

Charles Wesley

2. Abiding is trusting without worrying. To abide also means to remain stable or fixed. It means to wait expectantly and patiently.

3. Read Psalm 61:2-4.

   a. Verse 2 says, "From the end of the earth will I cry unto thee, when my heart is overwhelmed: lead me to the rock that is higher than I."

b. Verse 3 says, “For thou hast been a shelter for me, and a strong tower from the enemy.”

c. Verse 4 says, “I will abide in thy tabernacle for ever.”

4. No one should seek a trial, but if God says it is time for a trial, then abide in God and He in you. Also, do not stay in the trial when God says to move on. Your attitude, inability to learn, or prayerlessness can keep you in a trial longer than God originally intended. But remember whether you are in a trial or in the sunshine it is essential to abide in the Lord forever. Stay fixed in God no matter what you are experiencing.

5. Abiding in the Lord is to stay close to him and let the fulness of the Spirit have its full work in you. John 14:16 says, “And I will pray the Father, and he shall give you another Comforter, that he may *abide* with you for ever.” The Lord never leaves you during a trial, even though you may feel forsaken.

6. There was once a man who pastored a seashore church in England among the rough sailors, but they loved him and he loved the work. He was sickly and unwell most of the time, and good health finally left him. The doctor advised him to retreat to sunny southern Europe, and he prepared to sail. The last Sunday before leaving, although he had no strength to stand up and preach, he forced himself and preached among his weeping people. That evening, by the light of the setting sun, he wrote these words:
Abide with me, Fast falls the eventide;
The darkness deepens; Lord, with me abide;
When other helpers fail, and comforts flee,
Help of the helpless, O abide with me!

7. This same hymn came to the rescue of a disabled British submarine years ago. The British Press Association reported this strange incident: A British submarine lay disabled on the ocean floor. After two days, hope of raising her was abandoned. The crew on orders of the commanding officer began singing very prayerfully, *Abide With Me*. The officer explained to the men that they did not have long to live. There was no hope of outside aid, he said, because the surface searchers did not know the vessel's position.

   Sedative pills were distributed to the men to quiet their nerves. One sailor was affected more quickly than the others, and he swooned. He fell against a piece of equipment and set in motion the submarine's jammed surfacing mechanism. The submarine went to the surface and made port safely. This did not just happen. This was the hand of God answering their prayerful song, *Help of the helpless, O abide with me.*

   a. When there is none to help, God is there.

      i. Psalm 22:11 says, "Be not far from me; for trouble is near; for there is none to help."

      ii. Psalm 33:20 says, "Our soul waiteth for the Lord: he is our help and our shield."

      iii. Psalm 124:8 says, "Our help is in the name of the Lord, who made heaven and earth."

   b. His help does not depend upon who you are, but upon His promises. He has promised to help those in trouble, and He does care. Just stand on the Word; it is that powerful.

      i. "So shall my word be that goeth forth out of my mouth: it shall not return unto me void, but it shall accomplish that which I please, and it shall prosper in the thing whereto I sent it" (Isaiah 55:11).

ii. "Casting all your care upon him; for he careth for you" (I Peter 5:7).

B. Just stay put and wait on the Lord.

1. Richard Fuller, from *Thoughts for the Quiet Hour,* gives the following analogy. "'In fierce storms,' said an old seaman, 'we can do but one thing, there is only one way; we must put the ship in a certain position and keep her there.'

"This, Christian, is what you must do. Sometimes, like Paul, you can see neither sun nor stars, and no small tempest lies on you; and then you can do but one thing; there is only one way. Reason cannot help you. Past experiences give you no light. Even prayer fetches no consolation. Only a single course is left. You must put your soul in one position and keep it there. You must stay upon the Lord; and, come what may--winds, waves, cross seas, thunder, lightning, frowning rocks, roaring breakers--no matter what, you must lash yourself to the helm, and hold fast your confidence in God's faithfulness, His covenant engagement, His everlasting love in Christ Jesus."

2. Psalm 37:7 says, "*Rest* in the Lord, and wait patiently for him: fret not thyself because of him who prospereth in his way."

3. Read Psalm 62:1-8. Notice verses 2, 5, & 8.

a. Verse 2 says, "He only is my rock, and my salvation; he is my defence; I shall not be greatly moved."

b. Verse 5 says, "My soul, wait thou only upon God; for my expectation is from him."

c. Verse 8 says, "Trust in him at all times; ye people, pour out your heart before him: God is a refuge for us."

4. Isaiah 40:31 says, "But they that wait upon the Lord shall renew their strength; they shall mount up with wings as eagles; they shall run, and not be weary; and they shall walk, and not faint."

    a. Eagles fly more swiftly against a wind than in a gentle breeze.

    b. One writer wrote, "The eagle watches the dark clouds overhead filling the sky with blackness. He will sit perfectly still, turning one eye and the the other towards the storm as the forked lightnings play back and forth. He never moves a feather until he feels the first burst of the breeze. It is then that he knows the hurricane has struck him. With a scream he swings his breast to the storm. It is the storm itself that he uses to soar upward into the black sky. God wants this experience to take place in the lives of every one of His children. We can turn the storm clouds into a chariot."

5. Lamentations 3:25 says, "The Lord is good unto them that wait for him, to the soul that seeketh him."

6. "Therefore I will look unto the Lord; I will wait for the God of my salvation: my God will hear me. Rejoice not against me, O mine enemy: when I fall, I shall arise; when I sit in darkness, the Lord shall be a light unto me" (Micah 7:7-8).

7. Psalm 27:14 says, "Wait on the Lord: be of good courage, and he shall strengthen thine heart: wait, I say, on the Lord."

    a. When you do not know what to to, simply wait and do nothing. Wait till the fog clears away.

    b. Dr. James Vaughan says, "Waiting has four purposes. It practices the patience of faith. It gives time for preparation for the coming gift. it makes the blessing the sweeter when it arrives. It shows the sovereignity of God--to give just when and as He pleases."

C. Waiting and abiding in the Lord makes us pray with expectancy to Him. Read the following Scriptures:

1. "The Lord hath heard my supplication; the Lord will receive my prayer" (Psalm 6:9).

2. "Is any among you afflicted? let him him pray" (James 5:13).

3. Psalm 55:1, 4-6, 17 & 22.

    a. Verse 1 says, "Give ear to my prayer, O God; and hide not thyself from my supplication."

    b. Verses 4-6 says, "My heart is sore pained within me: and the terrors of death are fallen upon me. Fearfulness and trembling are come upon me, and horror hath overwhelmed me. And I said, Oh that I had wings like a dove! for then would I fly away, and be at rest."

    c. Verse 17 says, "Evening, and morning, and at noon, will I pray, and cry aloud: and he *shall* hear my voice."

d. Verse 22 says, "Cast thy burden upon the Lord, and he shall sustain thee: he shall never suffer the righteous to be moved."

4. Psalm 88:1-3 says, "O Lord God of my salvation, I have cried day and night before thee: Let my prayer come before thee: incline thine ear unto my cry; For my soul is full of troubles: and my life draweth nigh unto the grave."

D. The Lord is with you and will hear you. Prayer to God brings results.

1. "Thou drewest near in the day that I called upon thee: thou saidst, Fear not" (Lamentations 3:57).

2. If God is with you that is all you need. It does not matter if you are in the dark or not, if He is there. Mary Gardner Brainard wrote the following poem that says it well.
So I go on, not knowing,
I would not, if I might
I would rather walk in the dark with God
Than go alone in the light;
I would rather walk with Him by faith
Than walk alone by sight.

3. J.H. McConkey writes the following in his booklet entitled, *Prayer*. "Spend an hour upon the knees and let God put strength into them. The hard task and the difficulties you may have to face, the unpleasant circumstances, the disappointments which render the heart, the hopes which are crushed, the sorrows that seem to be constantly abiding, all can be lifted if God is given some of the time He requires of thee on the knees. The essence of praying is to get out of ourselves so that God can get in.

"Have you ever toyed with the key of a telegraph instrument while the circuit was closed? On that key you may write a complete message. Upon it every telegraphic character may be perfectly formed; every condition of expert operating may be fulfilled. But it matters not how skillful an operator you are, so long as the electric circuit is closed, all your efforts are simply sounding brass and clattering platinum. Not a single spark of electric life do you transmit. Why? Because the battery is not working. And all your working is effort without result, activity without power. Open the little brass lever which connects your key to the battery hidden beneath the table. Immediately every letter you form thrills with life, every word you write flashes a living message into the mind and heart of the far-away receiver. Though your work, dead and mechanical in itself, the electric battery is now pouring forth its vital stream, flooding with life and power every deft motion of your flying fingers.

"The lesson is plain. It is in spiritual telegraphy as in material. If the battery is not working the message is mere clatter. We may do, but if God is not doing through us then all our doing is naught. Prayer connects us with the divine battery of life and power. Prayer puts you 'in the Spirit,' and 'it is the Spirit that quickeneth.'"

4. Prayer works.

   a. Abraham's servant prays...Rebekah appears.

   b. Jacob wrestles and prays and Esau's mind is turned from its revengeful purpose.

   c. Joshua prays...Achan is discovered.

   d. Hannah prays...Samuel is born.

   e. Daniel prays...the lions are muzzled.

   f. Elijah prays...rain descends.

   g. The Church prays...Peter is delivered by an angel.

5. When you draw nigh to God and develop a relationship with Him, He will be there for you when you need Him. One of my favorite stories adapted from *A Message from God*, is a true story from Exeter, England. "A shabby old gentleman who every day at twelve o'clock would enter the church, stay a few minutes, then leave. The caretaker was concerned for the valuable furnishings. Every day he watched to be sure nothing was taken, and every day just at twelve the shabby figure would arrive. One day the caretaker accosted him. 'Look here, my friend, what are you up to, going into the church every day?'

"'I go to pray,' replied the old man politely.

"'Now come,' the cautious caretaker said, 'you don't stay very long to pray.'

"'True enough. I cannot pray a long prayer, but every day I just comes and says, 'Jesus, it's Jim.' Then I waits a minute, then comes away. I guess He hears me though it's but a little prayer.'

"One day Jim was knocked down crossing the street and was laid up in the hospital with a broken leg. The ward where Jim quite happily lay was a sore spot to the nurses on duty. Some of the men were cross and miserable, others did nothing but grumble from morning till night. Slowly but surely the men stopped their grumbling and were cheerful and contented.

"One day as the nurse was walking through the ward she heard the men laughing. 'What has happened to all of you? You are such a cheerful lot of patients lately.'

"'It's old Jim,' they replied, 'He's always cheerful, never complains, although he is uncomfortable and in pain.'

"The nurse walked over to Jim's bed where the silvery haired Jim lay with an angelic look on his smiling face. 'Well, Jim, these men say you are the cause for the change in this ward. They say you are always happy.'

"'Aye, that I am, nurse. I can't help it. You see, nurse, it's my visitor. He makes me happy.'

"'Visitor?' The nurse was indeed puzled for she had never noticed any visitor by Jim's bed. The chair was always empty during visiting hourse. 'When does your visitor come?'
"'Every day,' replied Jim with the light in his eyes growing brighter. 'Yup, every day at twelve o'clock He comes and stands at the foot of my bed. I see Him there, and He smiles at me and says, 'Jim, it's Jesus.''

Author unknown

D. Do not be bowed down but consider the Lord in all things.

1. "For consider him that endured such contradiction of sinners against himself, lest ye be wearied and faint in your minds" (Hebrews 12:3).

2. George Matheson writes, "What a strange cure for mental weariness. There is prescribed an increase of thought *'consider Him.'* I should have expected an invitation to mental rest. When a man's body is weary, we send him to sleep. When a man's mind is weary, why do we not also prescribe repose? Because the weariness of the mind needs an opposite cure from the weariness of the body. The weariness of the body is cured by slumber; but the weariness of the mind can be cured only by stimulus."

3. "*When we are flat on our back there is no way to look but up.*" Roger W. Babson

4. One night a terrible storm raged outside. The following morning the storm was gone, but there was dense fog. This is what can happen during a time of stormy trial in your life. Your mind can become so fogged you cannot see clearly. People walk and drive slower because of the density of the fog. There are many accidents in the fog. When you are in a situation that seems all fogged up, this is the best time to just abide in

God and consider Him. Let His Word be your guide and not your own thoughts.

5. Do not be like the children of Israel who did not consider the Lord. Isaiah 1:3 says, "My people doth not consider."

Lesson VI Quiz

1. What does it mean to abide in the Lord?

2. Why is it important to consider the Lord?

3. Name six people who encountered a difficulty and prayed. Give also the miracle that God did for them.

    a.

    b.

    c.

    d.

    e.

    f.

4. Quote Hebrews 12:3.

Women of the Spirit Bible Study

Learn in the Trial

Lesson VII

VII. Learn in the Trial

A. During the time of trial and lowliness woman can learn valuable lessons.

1. Jesus said in Matthew 11:28-29 to learn of him.

   a. "Come unto me, all ye that labour and are heavy laden, and I will give you rest."

   b. Take my yoke upon you, and *learn* of me; for I am meek and lowly in heart: and ye shall find rest unto your souls."

2. "Before I was afflicted I went astray: but now have I kept thy word" (Psalm 119:67).

3. "It is good for me that I have been afflicted; that I might *learn* thy statutes" (Psalm 119:71).

4. The time of trials help us to learn about tenderness, love, compassion, and patience. James H. McConkey writes in *Chastening*, the following: "The late summer showers are

falling. The poet stands by the window watching them. They are beating and buffeting the earth with their fierce downpour. But the poet sees in his imaginings more than the showers which are falling before his eyes. He sees myriads of lovely flowers which shall soon be breaking forth from the watered earth, filling it with matchless beauty and fragrance. And so he sings:

It isn't raining rain for me, it's raining daffodils;
In every dimpling drop I see wild flowers upon the hills.
A cloud of gray engulfs the day, and overwhelms the town:
It isn't raining rain for me; it's raining roses down.

"Perchance some one of God's chastened children is even now saying: 'O God, it is raining hard for me tonight. Testings are raining upon me which seem beyond my power to endure. Disappointments are raining fast, to the utter defeat of all my chosen plans. Bereavements are raining into my life which are making my shrinking heart quiver in its intensity of suffering. The rain of affliction is surely beating down upon my soul these days.' Withal, friend, you are mistaken. It isn't raining rain for you. It's raining blessing. For if you will but believe your Father's word, under that beating rain are springing up spiritual flowers of such fragrance and beauty as never before grew in that stormless, unchastened life of yours. You indeed see the rain. But, do you see, also, the flowers? It isn't raining afflictions for you. It is raining tenderness, love, compassion, patience and a thousand other flowers and fruits of the blessed Spirit which are bringing into your life such a spiritual enrichment as all the fullness of worldly prosperity and ease was never able to beget in your innermost soul."

5. Psalm 94:12 says, "Blessed is the man whom thou chastenest, O Lord, and teachest him out of thy law."

6. God is a deliverer and a teacher in the time of trouble. When David talked to the Lord in Psalm 32:7, the Lord responded in verse 8.

a. Verse 7 says, "Thou art my hiding place; thou shalt preserve me from trouble; thou shalt compass me about with songs of deliverance. Selah."

b. Selah means to pause and think. The writer is saying, "Reflect on what I just said for a moment."

c. "I (God) will *instruct* thee and *teach* thee in the way which thou shalt go: I will guide thee with mine eye."

B. Understanding, knowledge, and wisdom comes from God and His Word.

1. "And we know that the Son of God is come, and hath given us an understanding, that we may know him that is true, and we are in him that is true, even in his Son Jesus Christ. This is the true God, and eternal life" (I John 5:20).

2. "The entrance of thy words giveth light; it giveth understanding unto the simple" (Psalm 119:130).

3. Paul put a premium on gaining knowledge about the Lord. Philippians 3:8 says, "...I count all things but loss for the excellency of the knowledge of Christ Jesus my Lord: for whom I have suffered the loss of all things, and do count them but dung, that I may win Christ."

4. "The fear of the Lord is the beginning of wisdom: and the knowledge of the holy is understanding" (Proverbs 9:10).

C. Wise women realize the importance of knowledge and wisdom, and will seek after it instead of complaining and whining about the trial. The virtuous woman's mouth is filled with wisdom because she has sought after it. "She openeth her mouth with wisdom" (Proverbs 31:26).

1. "Wisdom is the principal thing; therefore get wisdom: and with all thy getting get understanding" (Proverbs 4:7).

2. "A wise man will hear, and will increase learning; and a man of understanding shall attain unto wise counsels. The fear of the Lord is the beginning of knowledge: but fools despise wisdom and instruction" (Proverbs 1:5, 7).

3. Read Proverbs 2:2-7. Notice especially the following verses.

    a. Verse 3 says, "Yes, if thou criest after knowledge, and liftest up thy voice for understanding;"

    b. Verse 4 says, "If thou seekest her as silver and searchest for her as for hid treasures;"

    c. Verse 5 says, "Then shalt thou understand the fear of the Lord, and find the knowledge of God."

    d. Verse 6 says, "For the Lord giveth wisdom: out of his mouth cometh knowledge and understanding."

4. Psalm 8:10-11 says, "Receive my instruction, and not silver; and knowledge rather than choice gold. For wisdom is better than rubies; and all the things that may be desired are not to be compared to it."

D. Greater things are seen by eyes that have been washed with tears.

1. April Oursler Armstrong relates how she learned this lesson. "As a child I was told that every cloud had a silver lining, that nothing happened without a reason, and that what seemed to be tragedy was, actually, a blessing in disguise. This was hard for my young mind to understand. As I grew older it became still harder to

understand, even though experience had given me my own practical proof of it.

"I remember my father, Fulton Oursler, sitting in his great library window with a storm-troubled bay framed behind him. I've forgotten now the cause of my 11-year-old grief, but it was to me severe sorrow. My father said: 'April, God sends the darkness of trouble not to punish us, but as a gift--even if we don't know why He gave it to us.'

"It was a time for darkness for him then, though I, in my ignorance, did not know it. Out of that darkness came his inspirational book on the life of Jesus, *The Greatest Story Ever Told.*

"As I grew older I learned for myself that darkness does indeed bring one closer to God. The illnesses of my own children, financial worries, loneliness, the death without warning of my parents, each of these things was a lesson in faith and love.

"But why? Why should God choose trouble as the path to Him?

"I found my answer in a book now lost, in a sentence I have come to live by. At first reading it seemed nonsense: 'Remember--you can see farther in the dark than in the day!'

"I read it again, and suddenly understood. In the dazzling light of day we cannot see beyond our own world. The sun that delights us keeps our eyes earthbound. But the night gently forces us to lift our eyes to the stars. You cannot see the stars in daylight. Nor can you see God so clearly in the noontime of happiness. It's not enough just to know in the daytime that the stars are still there. We know, but we forget them. If He did not send the night, we would not see the stars. If He did not send darkness to our lives, we might not ever see that we need Him—for light, for love, for joy. The secret is to open your eyes...to see in darkness as in light."

2. It was darkness that helped Isaiah see the Lord. "In the year that king Uzziah died I saw also the Lord sitting upon a throne, high and lifted up, and his train filled the temple" (Isaiah 6:1).

   a. When one sees the Lord, then the ugliness of self is revealed. "Then said I, Woe is me! for I am undone; because I am a man of unclean lips, and I dwell in the midst of a people of unclean lips: for mine eyes have seen the King, the Lord of hosts" (Isaiah 6:5).

   b. It was heartbreak and tears that brought about growth and cleansing in Isaiah and led him on to greater service. "Also I heard the voice of the Lord, saying, Whom shall I send, and who will go for us? Then said I, Here am I; send me" (Isaiah 6:8).

3. J.R. Miller writes in 1886 from *Silent Times*, the following: "It is in sorrow-darkened hearts where Christ truly dwells within. When Christ is within us, sorrow is a time of revelation. It is like the cloud that crowned the summit of the holy mountain into which Moses climbed, and by which he was hidden so long from the eyes of the people. While folded in the clouds, he was looking upon God's face. Sorrow's cloud hides the world, and wraps the wondering one in thick darkness; but in the darkness, Christ Himself unveils the splendor and glory of His face. There are many who never saw the beauty of Christ, and never knew Him in the intimacy of a personal friendship, till they saw Him, and learned to talk with Him as Friend with friend, in the hour of sorrow's darkness. When the lamps of earth went out, Christ's face appeared."

Lesson VII Quiz

1. Quote and explain Matthew 11:28-29.

2. Why does God choose affliction and suffering to teach his children?

3. Write out the following Scriptures:

    a. Proverbs 31:26.

    b. Psalms 8:10-11.

    c. Proverbs 4:7.

    d. Psalm 119:130.

    e. Psalm 119:67

Women of the Spirit Bible Study
Be Challenged
in the Trial
Lesson VIII

VIII. Be Challenged in the Trial

A. You have been challenged to fight.

1. Challenge is an invitation to engage in a contest; a summons to fight, to dare.

2. Paul says in I Corinthians 9:26-27, "I therefore so run, not as uncertainly; so fight I, not as one that beateth the air. But I keep under my body, and bring it into subjection."

3. The early Church waxed valiant in fight. "Hebrews 11:34, "Quenched the violence of fire, escaped the edge of the sword, out of weakness were made strong, waxed valiant in fight."

4. I Timothy 6:12 says, "Fight the good fight of faith, lay hold on eternal life, whereunto thou art also called."

5. The Christian walk is likened unto a soldier in warfare. II Timothy 2:3 says, "Thou therefore endure hardness, as a good soldier of Jesus Christ."

6. Spurgeon told the following story. "At the battle of Crecy, where Edward, the Black Prince, then a youth of eighteen years of age, led the van, the king, his father, drew up a strong party on a rising ground, and there beheld the conflict in readiness to send relief when it should be wanted. The young prince being sharply charged and in some danger, sent to his father for help; and as the king delayed to send it, another messenger was sent to crave immediate assistance. To him the king replied: 'Go, tell my son that I am not so inexperienced a commander as not to know when help is wanted, nor so careless a father as not to send it.' He intened the honor of the day should be his son's, and therefore let him with courage stand to it, assured that help should be had when it might conduce most to his renown. God draws forth His servants to fight in the spiritual warfare, where they are engaged, not only against the strongholds of carnal reason and the exalted imaginations of their own hearts, but also in the pitched field against Satan and his wicked instruments. But they, poor hearts, when the charge is sharp, are ready to respond with and cry with Peter: 'Save, Lord; we perish.' God is too watchful to overlook their exigencies, and too much a Father to neglect their help. If help, however, be delayed, it is that the victory may be more glorious by the difficulty of overcoming."

7. Paul said, "I have fought a good fight" (I Timothy 4:7). What was included in his fight? How did he feel about his trials and infirmities? Read II Corinthians 11:24-28, 30.

   a. Verse 24 says, "Of the Jews five times received I forty stripes save one."

   b. Verse 25 says, "Thrice was I beaten with rods, once was I stoned, thrice I suffered shipwreck, a night and a day I have been in the deep."

c. Verse 26 says, "In journeyings often, in perils of waters, in perils of robbers, in perils by mine own countrymen, in perils by the heathen, in perils in the city, in perils in the wilderness, in perils in the sea, in perils among false brethren."

d. Verse 27 says, "In weariness and painfulness, in watchings often, in hunger and thirst, in fastings often, in cold and nakedness."

e. Verse 28 says, "Besides those things that are without, that which cometh upon me daily, the care of all the churches."

f. Verse 30 says, "If I must needs glory, I will glory of the things which concern mine infirmities."

8. You can either give up to despair, or you can accept the challenge and be an inspiration in the trial, just as Paul was.

B. Challenge can accompany resistance.

1. Henry Van Dyke wrote, "No doubt a world in which matter never got out of place and became dirt, in which iron had no flaws and wood no cracks, in which gardens had no weeds, and food grew already cooked, in which clothes never wore out and washing was as easy as the soap makers' advertisements describe it, in which rules had no exceptions and things never went wrong, would be a much easier place to live in. But for purposes of training and development it would be worth nothing at all.

"It is the resistance that puts us on our mettle: it is the conquest of the reluctant stuff that educates the worker. I wish you enough difficulties to keep you well and make you strong and skillful."

2. *"The gem cannot be polished without friction, nor man perfected without trials."*

Chinese Proverb

3. Become the woman God wants you to be. Do not lie down and die, but come forth as gold. It is never to late to begin. Today is the first day of the rest of your life.

   a. Andrew R. Marker wrote a short essay entitled, *The Boy*. The following is that essay, but changed to *The Girl*. "A girl stood there, as I opened the door, whom I thought I'd seen somewhere before. 'What do you want, young lady?' said I, as she gazed at me with a puzzled eye.
   "'Excuse me,' she said, 'for troubling you; I'm seeking a friend that I once knew. You look like her, you bear her name, but now I see you're not the same. She used to live at this address, but she has moved away, I guess.'
   "And turning away, she left my place with disappointment in her face. With a 'Goodbye, ma'am,' she closed the gate, and left me there disconsolate.
   "And then I heard, as strange it seems, a voice I'd heard in my youthful dreams. An inner voice, that said to me: 'That girl is the girl you used to be! Her wistful heart has a pang within, for she's seeking the woman you might have been!'"

   b. *Don't Give Up.*
   'Twixt failure and success the point's so fine
   Women sometimes know not when they touch the line,
   Just when the pearl was waiting one more plunge,
   How many a struggler has thrown in the sponge!
   Then take this honey from the bitterest cup:
   "There is no failure save in giving up!"
   Author unknown

c. Read Psalm 84:5-7.

i. Verse 5 says, "Blessed is the man whose strength is in thee: in whose heart are the ways of them."

ii. Verse 6 says, "Who passing through the valley of Baca, make it a well; the rain also filleth the pools."

iii. Verse 7 says, "They go from strength to strength,every one of them in Zion appeareth before God."

iv. Baca means tears or weeping. Read it like this: "Blessed is the woman, who passing through the valley of tears, makes it a time of refreshing. It is a time of strength to her."

d. Queen Esther went through her time of weeping, but she leaned upon her God. She won a victory not only for herself, but for her people. She not only wept, but faced death by two counts: one because she was Jewish, and another because of the law which governed the golden sceptre of the king. Read Esther 4:11 & 16.

i. In verse 11, Esther is speaking to Hatach and commanded to tell Mordecai, "All the king's servants, and the people of the king's provinces, do know, that whosoever, whether man or woman, shall come unto the king into the inner court, who is not called, there is one law of his to put him to death, except such to whom the king shall hold out the golden sceptre, that he may live: but I have not been called to come in unto the king these thirty days."

ii. In verse 16 again Esther sends an answer to Mordecai, "Go, gather together all the Jews that are present in Shusan, and fast ye for me, and neither eat nor drink three days, night or day: I also and my maidens will fast likewise; and so will I go in unto the king, which is not according to the law: and if I perish, I perish."

iii. Prayer to God gave her the courage to stand before the king without being summoned, for she knew God was with her.

iv. The results of her courage was that she and Mordecai ruled in the kingdom and had great authority, while Haman was killed on the very gallows he had erected for Mordecai. See Esther 7:10.

v. Esther 9:29 says, "Then Esther the queen...wrote with all authority..." She went through her test and won a great victory.

C. Challenge can bring out the best in you.

1. Colton wrote, "Times of great calamity and confusion have ever been productive of the greatest minds. The purest ore is produced from the hottest furnace, and the brightest thunderbolt comes from the darkest storm."

2. "*Difficulties strengthen the mind, as labor does the body.*"

Seneca

3. The following excerpt was taken from *A Message from God.* "There are some natures that only a tempest can bring out. I recollect being strongly impressed on reading the account of an old castle in Germany with two towers that stood upright and far apart, between which an old

baron stretched large wires, thus making an Aeolian harp. There were the wires suspended, and the summer breezes played through them, but there was no vibration. Common winds, not having power enough to move them, split and went through them without a whistle. But when there came along great tempest winds, and the heaven was black, and the air resounded, then these winds, with giant touch, swept through the wires, which began to sing and roar, and pour out sublime melodies. So God stretches the chords in the human soul which under ordinary influences do not vibrate; but now and then great tempests sweep them through, and men are conscious that tones are produced in them which could not have been produced except by some such storm-handling."

4. "*Strength is born in the deep silence of long-suffering hearts*."

Felicia Hemans

D. Challenges, difficulties, troubles, and trials can be a blessing in disguise.

1. Samuel L. Brengle's little classic, *Helps to Holiness*, was originally written as a series of articles and penned during a period of convalescence after a tough kid threw a whole paving brick at the author's head. The Brengles used to say, "If there had been no little brick, There would have been no little book."

Mrs. Brengle kept the brick and painted a text on it. The text says, "But as for you, ye thought evil against me; but God meant it unto good, to bring to pass, as it is this day to save much people alive"(Genesis 50:20).

2. From the *Prairie Overcomer* came this story. "When Lord Clive, as a young man, in the spirit of adventure set out from his British home for India, the ship upon which he sailed was caught in a terrific storm. Continuous

adverse gales drove it far off the course, until it finally limped into a South American harbour. There he had to remain for many months before being able to get passage to India.

"But during the long wait he acquired the Portuguese language. This qualified him when he did reach India to take an important position with the East India Company, ultimately resulting in his being appointed by the crown as Governor General of India. *Do not deplore the upsets; they may be God's messengers.*"

Author unknown

3. W.W. Weeks shares the following story. "Years ago a fishing fleet went out from a small harbor on the east coast of Newfoundland. In the afternoon there came up a great storm. When night settled down not a single vessel of all the fleet had found its way into port. All night long wives, mothers, children, and sweethearts paced up and down the beach, wringing their hands and calling on God to save their loved ones. To add to the horror of the situation, one of the cottages caught fire. Since the men were all away, it was impossible to save the home.

   "When the morning broke, to the joy of all, the entire fleet found safe harbor in the bay. But there was one face which was a picture of despair–the wife of the man whose home had been destroyed. Meeting her husband as he landed, she cried, 'Oh, husband, we are ruined! Our home and all it contained was destroyed by fire!' But the man exclaimed,'Thank God for the fire! It was the light of our burning cottage that guided the whole fleet into port!'"

4. The Scriptures are filled with instances where something good came out of something bad.

   a. Because Daniel went to the lion's den, the people were made to serve his God. See Daniel 6:23-27.

b. Joseph had to go the route of the pit, prison, Potiphar's house before he went to the palace where he was used by God to save many people. See Genesis 37, 39, and 50:20.

c. Paul, who was forced to sit in prisons, wrote many of the epistles while there. See II Corinthians 11:23.

E. Nothing can stop you from accepting the challenge and overcoming your trials. The following people had difficulties, which they overcame. If they can do it, with the Lord's help, so can you.

1. "Here is a sensitive son of a poor preacher. He was regarded as a stupid blockhead in the village school. When he finally got a degree from college, he was the lowest on the list. He was rejected for the ministry. He tried law with the same result. He borrowed a suit of clothes to take an examination as a hospital mate, failed, and pawned his clothes. He lived in garrets, failing at everything he tried. Only one thing he wanted to do–write. This he did and rose above the handicaps of illness, poverty, and obscurity to high rank among the greatest writers of all time. His name was Oliver Goldsmith."

   Paul Lee Tan

2. "It is wonderful how many of the elect of the human race the winners of immortal fame entered the contest with a severe handicap. HOMER was a blind minstrel; and MILTON, too was blind, BEETHOVEN was deaf: 'Though so deaf he could not hear the thunder for a token, he made music of his soul, the grandest ever spoken.' ALEXANDER THE GREAT was a hunchback; SHAKESPEARE on his own testimony was a criple; and so were SCOTT, BRYON and KELVIN, to say nothing of EPICTETUS."

   Paul Lee Tan

3. “When a man [or woman] is determined, what can stop him [or her]? Cripple him and you have a SIR WALTER SCOTT; put him in a prison cell and you have a JOHN BUNYAN: bury him in the snows of Valley Forge and you have a GEORGE WASHINGTON. Have him born in abject poverty and you have a LINCOLN. Load him with bitter racial prejudice and you have a DISRAELI. Afflict him with asthma until as a boy he lies choking in his father's arms and you have a THEODORE ROOSEVELT; put him in a grease pit of a locomotive roundhouse and you have a WALTER CHRYSLER; make him a second fiddle in an obscure South American orchestra and you have a TOSCANNI.”

   Paul Lee Tan

4. “Blind men seldom quote books, but it is not so with Milton. The prodigious power, readiness, and accuracy of his memory, as well as the confidence he felt in it, are proved by his setting himself, several years after he had become totally blind, to compose his *Treatise on Christian Doctrine*, which, made up as it is of Scriptural texts, would seem to recquire perpetual reference to the Sacred Volume.

   “A still more extraordinary enterprise was that of the Latin Dictionary–a work which, one would imagine, might easily wear out a sound pair of eyes. After five years of blindness, he undertook these two vast works, along with *Paradise Lost*.”

   Julius C. Hare

5. When someone has the will, the way will mostly open itself. Francis Mouthelon, to whom was awarded the 1000 franc prize by the French society of artists for the loveliest painting in 1895, had no hands. He painted with a wooden hand.

6. An amazing story of sheer courage in the face of tremendous odds is that of Nancy Merki. Stricken with polio at 10, she was condemned to wear heavy braces and later crutches. Yet, in four years she became a swimming champion. When the President , asked how she had become the youngest champion despite infantile paralysis she answered, "Well, I guess I just kept trying, Mr. President."

7. George Frederick Handel, the great musician, lost his health; his right side was paralyzed; his money was gone; and his creditors seized and threatened to imprison him. Handel was so disheartened by his tragic experience that he almost despaired for a brief time. But his faith prevailed, and he composed his greatest work, "The Hallelujah Chorus," which is part of his great "Messiah."

8. The Apostle John wrote, "This is the victory that overcometh the world, even our faith" (I John 5:4). Many of the above stories were of sheer will power in the face of massive adversity to achieve that which would bless mankind. My question to you is this, "What excuse do you have for not overcoming trials victoriously, when the prize is much greater than the world's acclaim?"

9. It was President Theodore Roosevelt who said, "Far better it is to dare mighty things, to win glorious triumphs, even though checkered by failure, than to take rank with those poor spirits who neither enjoy much nor suffer much, because they live in the grey twilight that knows not victory nor defeat."

F. Now is the time to be strong, to get up and fight, and to forge ahead and win!

1. Paul said in Ephesians 6:10, "Be strong in the Lord, and in the power of his might."

2. Katherine Bevis tells how among the students at a well known college there was a young man who had to get around on crutches. He had an unusual friendly and optimistic disposition that won the deep respect of his classmates. One day a student asked him what had caused his deformity. “Infantile paralysis,” he replied briefly, not wishing to elaborate on his difficulties. “With a misfortune like that, how can you face the world so?” inquired his classmates. “Oh,” replied the young Christian, smiling, “the disease never touched my heart.”

3. The story of one of the great presidents of Harvard College, Charles William Eliot, was born with a serious facial disfigurement. He discovered as a young man that nothing could be done about it, and he must go through life with this mark. It is related that when his mother brought to him that tragic truth, it was indeed “the dark hour of his soul.” His mother told him, “My son, it is not possible for you to get rid of this handicap. We have consulted the best surgeons, and they say that nothing can be done. But it is possible for you, with God's help, to grow a mind and soul so big that people will forget to look at your face.”

4. Benjamin P. Browne writes about the incident that changed the outcome of World War II. “Days immediately after Dunkirk were darkest for the modern world. In supreme disaster, all seemed irrevocably lost and the invasion of England loomed imminent. England lay prostrate. Forty-seven warships had been sunk in the operations off Norway after Dunkirk. When the evacuation was completed, half the British destroyers were in the shipyards for repairs while the Royal Force had lost forty per cent of its bomber strength. Britain was on the brink of famine and her armies were without arms or equipment. They had left in France 50,000 vehicles.

“Churchill spoke for the defenseless islanders, ‘We shall defend our island whatever the cost may be; we shall fight on the beaches; we shall fight in the fields; we shall fight in the streets; and we shall fight in the hill. We shall never surrender and if this island were subjugated and starving, our empire on the seas would carry on the struggle until in God's good time the New World with all its power and might steps forth to the rescue and liberation of the old.'"

5. With God on your side you are guaranteed victory, so keep fighting and reaching ahead for greater things. If you are knocked down, get up and go again. If life knocks the breath out of you, breathe heaven's oxygen. Pray and touch divinity. You were born to succeed, not to fail.

6. The following scriptures will take you through any trial.

   a. "Now unto him that is able to do exceeding abundantly above all that we ask or think, according to the power that worketh in us" (Ephesians 3:20). The abundantly above God is on your side.

   b. "What shall we then say to these things? If God be for us, who can be against us?" (Romans 8:31).

   c. Read II Corinthians 4:15-18.

      i. Verse 15 says, "For all things are for your sakes, that the abundant grace might through the thanksgiving of many redound to the glory of God."

      ii. Verse 16 says, "For which cause we faint not; but though our outward man perish, yet the inward man is renewed day by day."

iii. Verse 17 says, "For our light affliction, which is but for a moment, worketh for us a far more exceeding and eternal weight of glory;"

iv. Verse 18 says, "While we look not at the things which are seen, but at the things which are not seen: for the things which are seen are temporal; but the things which are not seen are eternal."

d. "I can do all things through Christ which strengtheneth me" (Philippians 4:13).

e. "There hath no temptation taken you but such as is common to man: but God is faithful, who will not suffer you to he tempted above that ye are able; but will with the temptation also make a way to escape, that ye may be able to bear it" (I Corinthians 10:13). God knows your load limit.

f. "For we have not an high priest which cannot be touched with the feeling of our infirmities; but was in all points tempted like as we are, yet without sin. Let us therefore come boldly unto the throne of grace, that we may obtain mercy, and find grace to help in time of need" (Hebrews 4:15-16).

Lesson VIII Quiz

1. Write out the following Scriptures:

    a. I Corinthians 9:26-27

    b. II Timothy 2:3

    c. Ephesians 6:10

    d. II Corinthians 4:17

    e. I Corinthians 10:13

2. Give the name and accomplishment of four people who were challenged in the trial instead of being defeated.

    a.

    b.

    c.

    d.

3. How can you turn your trials into a triumph and let them be a challenge instead of a loss.

Women of the Spirit Bible Study

Vol. I: **Love, God's Way**

Vol. II: **Faith, Prayer, & Spiritual Warfare**

Vol. III: **All About Trials**

Vol. IV: **Wisdom, Attitudes, & Character**

These can be ordered from:

Radiant Life Publications
9025 N. West Lane
Stockton, CA 95210
Ph. 209-957-4027
Fax 209-476-7888